DEWEY F. BARTLETT

DEWEY F. BARTLETT
THE BARTLETT LEGACY

BY BOB BURKE

AND KENNY FRANKS

FOREWORD BY
UNITED STATES SENATOR SAM NUNN

VOLUME II
OKLAHOMA STATESMEN SERIES

SERIES EDITOR
GINI MOORE CAMPBELL

100 N. University, Edmond,
Oklahoma 73034

Libarary of Congress Catalog Number: 94-069823

ISBN 1-885596-01-4

A joint project of the University of Central Oklahoma and the Oklahoma Heritage Association, the Oklahoma Statesmen Series is dedicated to preserving the oral legacy of Oklahoma's great political leaders and their impact on state, national, and international affairs.

Oklahoma
Statesmen Series

FOREWORD

I had the great privilege of being a close friend and colleague of Dewey Bartlett in the United States Senate. I was deeply honored when Ann Bartlett asked me to write this Foreword.

Dewey and I came to the Senate together, in January 1973, and were both assigned to the Armed Services Committee and its Subcommittee on Manpower. We shared a strong interest in national security affairs and foreign policy issues, which was the first of many bonds between us.

Dewey, Lawton Chiles, Pete Domenici and I took part in an informal prayer luncheon each Wednesday that the Senate was in session. At those luncheons, we formed close spiritual bonds and a friendship that transcended differences of party or political philosophy.

Dewey accomplished a great deal in his six years in the Senate. His training as a geological engineer and background as a highly successful oil company executive were valuable when he became a key member of the Energy Committee during a period of energy crisis for the United States. He was acutely aware of the needs and concerns of the people in Oklahoma, and he worked closely with the Department of Housing and Urban Development and the Army Corps of Engineers to see that the rural areas of his state received federal services such as housing and flood control comparable to the services enjoyed by urban areas.

A proud retired Marine, he closely followed all important Marine Corps programs, and took the lead in ensuring that the Commandant of the Marine Corps was made a full-fledged member of the Joint Chiefs of Staff.

He and I collaborated on a report in the mid-1970s dealing with the Soviet military threat and the many inadequacies in NATO's ability to counter that threat. Unlike so many reports that come out of Congress, the report was widely read and had a major impact in bringing about the strengthening of the West's ability to deter and contain the Soviet Union during the critical years following the Vietnam War.

Dewey was a leader on arms control issues, frequently visiting the SALT II negotiations in Geneva and the nuclear weapons laboratories in the United States. He became an expert on the complex issue of nuclear testing.

His many successes in Oklahoma and the Senate bore witness to the personal qualities that marked the character of Dewey Bartlett. He was devoted to his wonderful wife, Ann, and their family. His core decency, instinctive consideration for others, and his rich, refreshing sense of humor helped to lighten many a person's load. He was deeply religious, and always put his country and his state above self.

Dewey Bartlett never will be forgotten by those of us who had the privilege of knowing and loving him. Through this book, a new generation will be better able to understand both the man and his impact on his time, and to see why I was proud to call him my good friend.

SAM NUNN

UNITED STATES SENATOR

PREFACE

The decision of Dewey Bartlett to adopt Oklahoma as his home state was great for both Bartlett and for Oklahoma. No political figure in the state's history has worked more tirelessly and unselfishly for the good of the people than Dewey Bartlett. He was a Republican when it was not popular to be a Republican. He worked hard to improve energy policies in America when that cause was not popular. The bottom line for Bartlett was—is it right for Oklahoma?

Bartlett's integrity was unquestioned. He had a high sense of ethics in government. He paid for trips from personal funds and once fired a Republican highway commissioner for improper campaign fund raising.

He had an incredible grasp of the world political stage. He was one of the few national leaders who warned America of the eventual conflict in the Persian Gulf.

We owe thanks to many people for making this book possible. Bartlett's widow, Ann Bartlett Burke, has been gracious in opening her home to look at stacks of photographs and scrapbooks. The staff at the Oklahoma State Library was superb in locating documents in the archives. Oral historian Rodger Harris at the Oklahoma Historical Society provided taped interviews of Governor Bartlett. United States District Judge Ralph Thompson and David Russell provided photos. Judge Thompson and former Bartlett Press Secretary Mike McCarville reviewed the manuscript. Research assistants Eric Dabney, Debi Engles, and Chimene Wood worked diligently and efficiently as usual.

Special thanks go to George Nigh, President of the

University of Central Oklahoma; Carl Reherman, Executive Director, Nigh Institute of State Government at UCO; J.M. "Jack" Graves, President, and Paul Lambert, Executive Director, Oklahoma Heritage Association and to Series Editor Gini Moore Campbell who keeps us all organized.

The grammar, spelling, punctuation, and capitalization in this volume is as it appears in the original documents. The only additions made by the authors are in the identification of individuals and locations and for clarification. These additions are set off by brackets.

BOB BURKE
KENNY FRANKS

TABLE OF CONTENTS

DEWEY F. BARTLETT

BORN AN OILMAN

Dewey Follett Bartlett was destined to be an oilman. The Bartlett family already had been consumed with oil fever for two generations when Dewey was born on a crisp spring morning in Marietta, Ohio, on March 28, 1919. The new baby boy was the talk of the town. His grandparents were among the most prominent and oldest families in Marietta.

David Albert Bartlett and Jessie Follett were married on the day after Christmas in 1916 in what a local newspaper described as one of the largest weddings in the history of southern Ohio. It was his second marriage, his first wife had died.

As the twentieth century began David already was recognized as a leader in America's infant oil industry. He had arrived in Marietta in 1901 and established a successful bank, one of the first in America to lend money for oil exploration, early the next year. His hunger for the oil patch came from his father, Benjamin F. Bartlett. The Bartletts moved from David's native New Hampshire to western Pennsylvania and on to West Virginia looking for oil. After settling in Marietta David heard about the oil boom in the Cherokee Nation, what is now northeast Oklahoma. He traveled to Bartlesville and Tulsa in 1902 and recognized the unlimited opportunities of the new oil and gas frontier in Indian Territory.

For hundreds of years before the Cherokees arrived in Oklahoma via the Trail of Tears, Plains Indians had used the black liquid that oozed between the rocks and accumulated on the surface of springs to cure rheumatism and other ailments and to treat cuts on themselves and their animals. The oil business in the future state of Oklahoma was given a major boost in 1897 when the search for oil produced Oklahoma's first commercially successful oil well, the Nellie Johnstone No. 1, along the bank of the Caney River near Bartlesville. The discovery was part of what would later be called the Mid-Continent Oil and Gas Region, a vast area of oil and gas reservoirs stretching from southeast Kansas, through Oklahoma into east Texas. By the time David Bartlett married Jessie Follett in 1916 he had accumulated large oil and gas holdings in Oklahoma even though he continued to live and run his bank in Ohio. In 1909 he was part of a group that bought the Deep Fork Oil Company in Okmulgee County. Two years later he was elected president of the Akin Oil Company in Tulsa. Akin Oil became a major player in the Oklahoma oil industry and was the owner of the first well to produce from the Wilcox Sand. The company also built two gasoline plants in Washington County, Oklahoma, and developed a large production in the Cushing Field.

The Follett side of the family had lived in Marietta for most of the nineteenth century. Jessie Follett was the third generation of her family to be born in Marietta. The Folletts were well-bred and well-educated. Jessie attended finishing school in New York City and studied in Rome and Paris. Jessie's father, Alfred Dewey Follett, graduated from Cornell University in Ithaca, New York, and practiced law with his father, Martin Dewey Follett, in Marietta. The younger Follett also served as a judge of the Supreme Court of Ohio and was an original investor in The Peoples Banking and Trust Company, the bank started by David A. Bartlett. Follett was a strong Democratic leader in southern Ohio and was a member of the Democratic State Executive Committee. He was known as Dewey Follett and his death in Marietta the day before election day in 1918 was prominently reported in the local newspaper which declared, "Ohio politics lost a lovable character."

Dewey died as he was raising the American flag in celebration of the armistice ending World War I. He fell, according to the newspaper account, "with the banner in his arms." The newspaper continued, "Politics was his relaxation. He loved a scrap only for the fun of contesting with his adversaries. Law, politics and society sustained a loss when he passed on to eternity with the flag he always patriotically supported draped about his falling form."

Dewey Bartlett at age one with his father, David Albert Bartlett.

Dewey would never get to know his successful father. David A. Bartlett died on Dewey's third birthday in 1922, leaving Jessie Bartlett with two small children, Dewey, and four-year-old David A. Bartlett Jr. By the time of his death, the elder Bartlett had organized the Keener Oil and Gas Company in Ohio, of which he served as president. This along with the other Oklahoma companies that held the Bartlett interests in the Sooner State left his family financially stable. Following his death, John McCoy, a longtime family friend from Marietta, took over the reins of the Bartlett production that by now spanned half the continent, from West Virginia to Oklahoma.

David Jr., he would be known throughout his life as Dave, graduated with a degree in petroleum engineering from the Massachusetts Institute of Technology in Cambridge, Massachusetts, and became president of Keener Oil and Gas Company in 1939. While at M.I.T. Dave developed an interest in water flooding oil fields that had exhausted production with normal pumping. Called secondary recovery, the procedure involved injecting pressurized water along one side of a producing formation. As the water moved through the formation it pushed oil before it. When the oil reached the other side of the formation it was pumped to the surface, thus allowing oilmen to tap the crude left behind by flush production. To learn the practical side of the oil industry Dave worked as a roustabout for Phillips Petroleum Company in Nowata County, Oklahoma during his summers at M.I.T.

While his brother completed college, Dewey attended public schools in Marietta and then transferred to Lawrenceville Prep, a prestigious preparatory school in Lawrenceville, New Jersey, where he was a starter on the school's basketball team. In 1938 Dewey enrolled at Princeton University in Princeton, New Jersey. Studying geological engineering, and played varsity basketball for three years. He also had his first brush with Oklahoma, the state that he would someday govern. In the summers of 1940 and 1941, he came west to work in the Oklahoma oil fields around Dewey, Bartlesville, and Konawa. Staying at the YMCA in Bartlesville, he packed his lunch everyday from the restaurant of the old Dewey Hotel where his father had headquartered on his pioneer trips to Oklahoma in 1902.

Dewey enlisted in the Navy in January before his graduation from Princeton in June, 1942, and was ordered to active duty immediately after graduation. Oklahoma again played a major role in his future. He received flight training at the Naval Air School in Norman. After receiving his wings and a commission as a second lieutenant he served as a dive bomber pilot in the Marine Corps for three and a half years. Leading numerous raids on Japanese targets in the South Pacific, he was awarded the Air Medal for outstanding combat duty. At the end of the war Dewey joined the Marine Corps Reserve and rose to the rank of captain.

Dewey's biggest coup was not against the Japanese but with a beautiful young girl named Ann Smith. They met at a USO dance at Laguna Beach, California, while Dewey was stationed at nearby El Toro Marine Air Station on his way overseas. Ann was reared in Seattle, Washington, where she attended both the University of Washington and Seattle University. After a whirlwind courtship, they fell deeply in love. When Dewey returned from his 18-month tour of duty they were married on April 2, 1945, in California's historic San Juan Capistrano mission.

Dewey and Ann moved to Tulsa in January, 1946. He quickly became active in the affairs of the family oil and gas business and put his geological engineering degree to work in expanding Keener Oil and Gas Company's production in Oklahoma and several other states. In December, 1951, Keener Oil and Gas Company was reorganized as Keener Oil Company, a partnership between Dewey, his brother, Dave, their mother, Jessie, and nephew, Lewis. Dewey and Dave became managing partners of the company that took over the multi-state holdings of the old Keener Oil and Gas Company.

Under this direction, Keener pioneered successful water flooding operations in the oil fields in Washington County. The company grew tremendously in the 1950s and by the middle of the decade employed more than 100 people who oversaw water flooding operations on more than 4,000 acres in Washington County. It also had interests in almost 600 oil wells. Dewey became Chairman of the Board of Dewey Supply Company, a retail oil field supply business with stores in Dewey, Chickasha, Ada, Oklahoma City, and Tulsa before it was acquired by Keener Oil in 1953. Dewey also helped form the Oklahoma Independent Producers Association and served as a charter board member.

BECOMING A PUBLIC SERVANT

Dewey adopted his mother's Republican political convictions early in life. He strongly believed in America's free market system and actively promoted the idea that private business could do most jobs more efficiently than big government. His first interest in politics came in Dwight D. Eisenhower's campaign for president in 1952, in which he served as a Republican precinct chairman in Tulsa. His hard work paid off. The precinct he chaired had the highest winning percentage for the Eisenhower-Nixon ticket of all precincts in Tulsa County.

Ironically, a bout with hepatitis influenced Dewey Bartlett to get more involved in politics. While recovering from hepatitis contracted on a family trip to Europe in 1960, he began reading books on American political history. As his interest grew, he volunteered to serve on a committee in 1962 to draft an opponent for the Democratic state senator in Tulsa County. When the committee could not find anyone to run, Dewey decided to enter the race himself. As he later recalled he looked at himself in the mirror one morning and said, "If I have guts enough to ask someone else to run, I ought to consider it myself." Asking his daughter Joanie what she thought about it, she said, "Go for it daddy." Dewey warned that he might lose but Joanie replied, "Well tough bazookies." The point was well taken. Dewey knew he was old enough at 42 to accept the hazards of politics. His brother Dave, a former chairman of the Republican State Finance Committee, also encouraged him to run for the Tulsa County senate seat. Both had worked hard in several Republican campaigns in the 1950s and Dewey knew most of the influential people in

Tulsa because of his active involvement in civic affairs. He had served as a board member for the YMCA, American Red Cross, Salvation Army, Young Christian Students, and Citizens for Constitutional Reapportionment.

Dewey announced his candidacy for the Republican nomination for the Oklahoma Senate on February 1, 1962. His message was simple. Oklahoma must have a viable two-party system or progress in the state would be stymied, a plea that was strengthened by the bitter fight between Democratic Governor J. Howard Edmondson and the Democratic legislature over the issue of reapportionment. The rural-dominated legislature resisted any effort to give more house and senate seats to Oklahoma City and Tulsa. Oklahoma and Tulsa Counties had only one seat each in the senate. A federal court in August, 1962, mandated apportionment of legislative seats by population on a one-man, one-vote basis. The ruling was a great victory for the cities. Tulsa County's representation in the State Senate rose from one senator to seven.

The cry for more Republicans in state government was at the center of Dewey's campaign. On reapportionment Dewey said, "Our state constitution has for all practical purposes been thrown in the ash can. This is a time for action. The only hope for true reform is the election of Republicans to state offices. Reform cannot come through the Democratic party because of the control of the Senate by the old guard clique."

Dewey faced the 66-year-old former Republican senator Arthur Price in the primary. Price had been swept out of office in 1958 when Democrat Yates Land rode the coat tails of J. Howard Edmondson's landslide victory. Dewey adopted a four-point program for progress: constitutional reapportionment, the elimination of earmarking of state funds, equalization of property tax assessments, and increased school consolidation.

When the votes were counted in the May 1 primary, Dewey won handily over Price. Senator Land easily captured renomination as a Democrat even though he had been stricken with cancer and campaigned sporadically. Tulsa newspapers predicted a close general election race. However, Senator Land died in September and Paul A. Walker Jr., a former Common Pleas Court judge, was selected to replace Land as the Democratic nominee.

Opposition to a proposed increase in the state sales tax mushroomed into a major campaign issue for Oklahoma Republicans. The proposal had come from Democratic gubernatorial nominee W.P. "Bill" Atkinson who wanted to raise the sales tax by one penny to increase funding for education and to spur economic development. Dewey opposed the sales tax hike and criticized Atkinson for preferring a tax increase over reduction in the size of state government. "It's a sad but true fact," he reminded voters, "that in Oklahoma we have 10.1 state employees per 1,000 population while Texas gets along with just 6.5 employees per 1,000 population. It's not as funny as it sounds to admit that it takes 101 Oklahomans to do the job of 65 Texans."

The November 6 general election was historic. Oklahoma elected its first Republican governor in history in Henry Bellmon, a farmer from Billings. Dewey won the Tulsa County State Senate seat, 49,299 to 38,956, getting more votes than Bellmon did in Tulsa County. Another political newcomer, David Hall, was elected to a full term as Tulsa's County Attorney. The two politicians were destined to meet on the Oklahoma political battlefield later.

Dewey hit the ground running as a state senator. He introduced 23 bills, among them measures to equalize property taxes and to give school districts more latitude in raising local taxes for support of education. He continued to fight for reapportionment of the legislature. The press took note of the new senator from Tulsa. *The Daily Oklahoman* declared Dewey "was a man to be reckoned with," and *Tulsa Tribune* reporter Frosty Troy said, "Few freshman senators have ever come on so strong in so short a time." Travis Walsh of the *Tulsa World* observed that Dewey was handicapped because he was one of only six Republican senators pitted against 38 Democrats. However, according to Walsh, Dewey had overcome his handicap with a blend of ability, hard work, dogged persistence and a pleasant personality.

The legislature completed drawing the legislative redistricting boundary lines in time for the 1964 elections. Even though Dewey had two years to go on his term, the reapportionment decision forced him to run for re-election. He ran in a newly carved District 39 and easily defeated Democrat W.P. Pitcock Jr., an electrical contractor.

Dewey continued to impress veteran politicians and the press. Although he often was mentioned as a possible successor to Governor Henry Bellmon, he initially resisted any efforts to seek higher office, a decision based on a meeting with Bellmon one night about 7:00 p.m. "I came into the side door of the office," he recalled, "and found the governor sitting there erect and asleep. I knew he was worn out with everything he was doing. I decided at that point I never wanted to be governor."

Dewey changed his mind in early 1966. He wanted to make a difference in Oklahoma's future and believed he could have a larger impact as governor than as a state senator. Republicans had been devastated by the Lyndon Johnson trouncing of Barry Goldwater in 1964. Dewey said the GOP only had two ways to go. One way was down and out and the other was to snap back. He pledged his efforts on the latter choice.

In announcing his candidacy for governor Dewey handed newsmen a 16-page platform called a "Program of Excellence." It called for non-partisan selection of judges, establishment of area vocational-technical schools, a junior college for Oklahoma City and Tulsa, encouragement of expansion and diversification of industry, and appointment of a commission to recommend judicial appointments.

Dewey was the first Catholic to mount a serious campaign for governor in Oklahoma. Believing that religion would not be a significant factor in the race, he resisted efforts to make religion a campaign issue. Other Republicans expressed concern that the prejudice against John F. Kennedy in the 1960 presidential election was still a silent factor among Protestants six years later. The election night outcome proved Dewey's decision to be the correct one.

The first hurdle Dewey had to clear in his drive for the governor's mansion was the Republican primary where he faced Bruno H. Miller and popular Waukomis banker and 20-year veteran state house member, John N. "Happy" Camp. The *Tulsa Tribune* announced its endorsement of Dewey in an editorial February 16:

> Our times demand another honest man with a keen mind, a good heart and willing hands. Bartlett has authored the 10 mill levy measure which has rescued dozens of public school districts from financial chaos. The eight bills which wiped Jim Crow laws off the books were his. While cynics said he could never do it, he secured Senate passage of measures to eliminate the silent vote and shorten the state ballot. One

> of the best tributes paid him came from a legislative leader who said: 'He will call you at midnight, he will camp in your office, he will drive you crazy if he thinks there's something wrong that the legislature could correct. He never quits.' Bartlett, in fact, had a perfect record on roll calls during the session. He possesses an opinion of his own. He has succeeded in living above the fog that blinds so many men who enter public service with a will and leave it with a whimper.

The campaign was put on hold momentarily when the sad news came in March from Ohio that Dewey's mother Jessie Bartlett Noll had died at age 79.

Resuming the campaign trail, Dewey made education the cornerstone of his race for governor. "As education goes, so Oklahoma will go," was his theme. He was haunted by the statistics that out of every 100 Oklahoma children who entered school, only 61 would graduate from high school and only 15 would graduate from college. Calling for upgrading schools and providing junior colleges and vo-tech schools, he argued that, "Education is the key to more jobs and better pay."

The theme of education and jobs rang true with Oklahoma's voters. Dewey ran first in the field of three, winning by less than 1,000 votes over Camp. However, Miller received 2,000 votes and forced the race into a runoff between Dewey and Camp. Dewey campaigned hard and widened the gap in the May 24th runoff. Dewey defeated Camp 49,916 to 38,043.

Ann Bartlett and the three children supported Dewey's run for governor enthusiastically. She daily attended teas and rallies and fundraisers. *The Sunday Oklahoman* profiled her efforts in the campaign as "The pretty, brown-haired Mrs. Bartlett, who looks little older than her daughter," and who "confessed, 'I don't give talks, I just go and see the people.' " "She stuffs envelopes, answers phone calls, and supports her husband. She prefers casual clothes because of the hectic campaign schedule by plane and car from sunup to midnight. She always has a smile for everyone she meets."

Preston J. Moore beat former governor Raymond Gary for the Democratic nomination in a traditionally bitter primary. Moore, who had a boyhood dream of becoming governor, had run unsuccessfully in 1962 but four years later clearly was the frontrunner.

Dewey, as a Republican, began at least 25 points behind in the early polls but by September state newspapers were predicting a much closer race. Believing in his message he continued to focus on jobs and education issues. The hard work, combined with Dewey's likeable personality, paid off. One Democratic legislator said, "You can't help but like him. Every time we knock him down, he gets up and tries again and never gets mad."

On Ann Bartlett's 46th birthday, November 8, her husband was elected Oklahoma's 19th governor, defeating Moore 377,078 to 296,328. Many attributed his win to the unpopularity of President Lyndon Johnson in Oklahoma while others said the election was a classic battle between rural and urban Oklahoma. Election returns supported the latter argument. Moore led Dewey in 40 of the state's 77 counties. However, Moore's 35,000 vote lead in rural counties could not overcome Dewey's landslide victory in Oklahoma and Tulsa counties. Dewey won Tulsa County by 40,000 votes and piled up 27,000 more votes than Moore in Oklahoma County.

The *Washington Post* called Dewey's victory "the end of political religious bigotry in Oklahoma." While the newly elected governor hailed his election as "another step toward a two-party system" in the state, Ann best summarized the election as she sat in the corner of a crowded ballroom at the Oklahoma City Sheraton Hotel on election night. "People don't really know Dewey the way I do," she stated. "When they see his quiet manner, they think of him as shy and many times are surprised at his determination." "The determination, however," the governor-elect's wife continued, "was the difference in this race." "I would like to believe that the good people of Oklahoma finally discovered the kind of man he is and this more than anything else was responsible for the victory." She concluded, "The victory is the most wonderful birthday present I will ever get."

The *Tulsa Tribune*, the morning after the election, said the victory was due to Dewey's endorsement by the Bellmon administration. The paper said, "Republicanism was tried and found wonderful. Fifty years of Democratic cobwebs were cleared out of the statehouse."

GOVERNOR BARTLETT

Dewey Bartlett tackled the job of running a state as he had all other tasks in his life, with fascinating determination. He immediately put together a transition team, naming statewide campaign coordinator Wayne Rowley as his administrative assistant. They plunged into details about every subject imaginable from the inauguration to dealing with a Democratic legislature.

Even before the inauguration Dewey met with House Speaker Rex Privett and Senate President Pro Tem Clem McSpadden, and even bought a bull from McSpadden for the 200-acre Bartlett ranch in Tulsa County. Dewey emerged from the meeting convinced that the "climate was great for good cooperation." Dewey moved into a State Capitol office to familiarize himself with the trappings of the Governor's Office. He appointed a special committee to study ad valorem tax equalization and traveled to New York City with Governor Bellmon to meet with some of the nation's most important industrial leaders to sell Oklahoma as the site for new plants and industries.

Dewey Follett Bartlett was inaugurated as Oklahoma's 19th governor January 9, 1967. His inaugural address sounded the call for Oklahomans to be proud of their state, of their families, and of themselves:

> Wherever you are, look around you. Look at your job, your home, yourself, your community, your state. I challenge you to set a new standard of excellence for yourself. Hold to that standard out of your pride in being an Oklahoman. I challenge you to set new, higher standards for those in your government. By letter, by telephone,

> wherever we meet, demand that we live up to those standards. And we will.

The new governor addressed the Oklahoma legislature the day after his inauguration. He followed through on his campaign promise to ask for more funding for common schools and higher education. Two-thirds of the requested budget increase was designated for education. He proposed the formation of a new Department of Corrections to deal with Oklahoma's growing problem of too many criminals and not enough cells to hold them. The new agency was quickly approved and innovative programs such as pre-release centers for inmates were introduced to cut the recidivism rate.

Dewey believed that running a state government was similar to running his own company. He did not gather around him a select group or "kitchen cabinet" or "brain trust." He operated on the theory that government could work if there was a friendly exchange with the legislature and other public officials. He met for breakfast with legislative leaders each Monday morning during a legislative session. He relied on the opinions of several people in deciding an issue, rather than lean heavily on any one individual.

Early in his administration Dewey asked private business in Oklahoma to study state government to look for ways to make the government more efficient. Business leaders, led by oil company executive Jimmy Allison, pledged more than $70,000 to fund the study that made far-reaching recommendations on restructuring and streamlining state government. It was estimated that the study's recommendations that were adopted saved the state 20-million dollars during the Bartlett administration. Possibly the most significant improvement in state government brought by the blue-ribbon panel's recommendations was in the area of investment of state money. The state received millions of dollars in additional interest each year after new methods of investing state funds were implemented.

Governor Bartlett fought increasing pressures for a massive tax increase. His pledge for educational improvement was difficult to attain without additional tax revenues. A massive student demonstration on the south steps of the state capitol building in the spring of 1967 focused attention on Oklahoma's higher education system. A hike in out-of-state tuition and the streamlining of higher education administration compensated for the lack of new tax money to finance

Dewey (r) and older brother David, Atlantic City, 1921.

increases suggested by the governor.

Oklahoma voters went to the polls in 1967 and approved a major overhaul of the state's judicial system. The Justice of the Peace system was eliminated and a new system of district courts and a change in the method of selecting judges came in the wake of several years of scandals involving even justices of the state's highest court.

Dewey was Oklahoma's favorite son candidate for President of the United States at the 1968 Republican National Convention. He withdrew his candidacy and threw his support behind the eventual winner, Richard M. Nixon. About Nixon, he said, "Though this loyal American knows Oklahoma and Oklahomans, the important qualification he possesses is that he knows each state, and its citizens...He knows America and Americans. I want a winner and Nixon is the man."

A "Pride in Oklahoma" campaign was unveiled by Governor Bartlett in 1968. It proved to be one of the most innovative and successful public relations efforts ever launched on behalf of a state. An Oklahoma City advertising agency in charge of industrial development approached the governor with plans to promote the state with advertising and bumper stickers and what would soon be the famous "Okie pin." The idea was to use the derogatory title given to Oklahomans by John Steinbeck in his novel *The Grapes of Wrath* to stress how far Oklahoma had come in its first 60 years. The initials O.K.I.E. stood for Oklahoma, Key to Intelligence and Enterprise; Oklahoma, Key to Industrial Expansion; or Oklahoma, Key to Individual Enthusiasm.

The OKIE program and the OKIE pin became the symbol of Dewey's pledge for an all-out effort of industrial development in Oklahoma. He said, "The OKIE program is meant to represent today's Oklahoma—a state filled with aggressive, willing to work and well-educated people who offer a day's work for a day's pay. There was a time", the govenor continued, "when if someone called you an Okie, you had better be pretty big or a good runner. We are trying to change that. We are trying to stir pride in Oklahoma by turning a dust bowl epithet into a modern day theme."

Throughout 1970 Governor Bartlett and the legislature continued to feud over tax reform. It was a matter of semantics. The governor thought the legislature was trying to quickly push through "tax increases" disguised as "tax reforms." Bartlett told the Oklahoma Press Association in January, 1970:

> I am not opposed to tax reform. I am opposed to a tax increase labeled as tax reform. The term tax reform means different things to different persons. To some, it means a tax increase. To others, it means a tax reduction. Still others consider it a tax directed at someone else. To me, it has a different meaning. To me, true tax reform means to change existing laws to accomplish a more equitable distribution of the tax burden, a simpler method of paying taxes, or a more efficient and fair method of tax collection, without at the same time increasing the overall tax burden. True tax reform takes time. It cannot be accomplished in a few months.

Bartlett also made advancement of minorities a cornerstone of his administration. He actively sought out minorities for public service. An American Indian, Don Bluejacket of Miami, was enlisted to work on minority affairs and became one of Bartlett's most valued advisers. Both Dewey and Ann worked tirelessly to promote and assist minority-owned businesses in the state.

The Bartlett family unanimously decided that Dewey should run for re-election in 1970. He drew no Republican opponent and saved his campaign war chest for an expected bitter battle with the Democratic nominee. County Attorney David Hall of Tulsa outdistanced Bryce Baggett, Joe Cannon, and Wilburn Cartwright in the Democratic primary.

The Bartlett-Hall race heated up quickly. There were only two months between the Democratic runoff in September and the general election in November. Hall, a charismatic campaigner, was determined to unseat Bartlett and re-establish the Democrats in the Governor's Mansion.

It was the closest governor's race in Oklahoma history. Hall defeated Dewey by slightly more than 2,000 votes, 338,338 to 336,157. American party candidate Reuel Little received 24,295 votes. A costly recount of the votes failed to change the verdict. Later, Dewey would reflect on his defeat, "I lost by less than one vote per precinct. I failed to realize that there was apathy for a Republican in a statewide race. There were no burning issues. It was simply Democrat versus Republican in an overwhelmingly Democratic state. I simply failed to get out the voters who thought I had done a good job as governor."

Dewey summed up his four years' accomplishments as governor in his State of the State message on January 5, 1971:

> Because of an embryo two-party system—not in spite of it—we have had a competitive yet harmonious relationship. 56 vetoes with only 3 final overrides attests to this fact. For the first in Oklahoma history, the available labor force passed the one million mark. We have had phenomenal growth and expansion of our economy. There is new enthusiasm in rural Oklahoma, an

> enthusiasm that is generated by a proven ability to attract industry and job opportunities.

Dewey was proud of his record on civil rights in his administration. A state Civil Rights Act was passed by the legislature. The first five African-American Oklahoma Highway Patrol officers were named, the first African-American state district judge, Charles Owens, was appointed, and African-Americans were appointed for the first time to the Oklahoma State University Board of Regents and the Tulsa Junior College Board of Regents. In addition, the Oklahoma Indian Affairs Commission was established.

One of the Hallmarks of the Bartlett administration was the unprecedented support of common education. Legislative appropriations increased by 89 percent in his four years. For the first time, state monies were designated for school counselors, special education, and kindergartens. Higher education appropriations jumped by 66 percent in the Bartlett administration. For the first time in 50 years, a new state-supported college, Tulsa Junior College, opened its doors. Vocational-technical schools increased from 4 to 15 in four years and vo-tech appropriations were up 112 percent. Dewey believed that a well-trained workforce was one of the best tools for attracting industry to Oklahoma.

Governor Bartlett, second from left, at the Tulsa Press Club, February, 1969.

MR. BARTLETT GOES TO WASHINGTON

After leaving the Governor's Mansion in early 1971, Dewey and Ann returned to their home in Tulsa and resumed a near-normal life. Dewey plunged into his work at Keener Oil but constantly thought about how much he had enjoyed serving the people of his adopted state.

In 1972, after much thought and consideration, he jumped into the race for the United States Senate seat vacated by Fred Harris. Harris was the first United States Senator from Oklahoma in 30 years to not seek re-election. He had opted to run for the Democratic nomination for President that year. When he dropped out of the presidential race, Harris stayed out of the race for his successor in Oklahoma.

Dewey had learned valuable lessons from the defeat in 1970. Campaign aide Mike McCarville recalls how different Dewey approached the 1972 race:

> He became a much tougher person after the defeat. In 1970, he had been content to let things ride along, confident that the voters would recognize what he had done and was trying to do. In the 1972 campaign, we spent most of our time telling voters what he had done as governor. He had always been a hard worker but absolutely drove all of us into the ground in the 1972 campaign. Twenty-two hour days were not uncommon. He often called in the wee hours of the morning to review the previous day's events and speculate about the days to come.

Dewey easily gained the Republican nomination by

trouncing political unknown C.W. Wood 94,935 to 7,029. The general election was a different story.

Eleven Democrats vied for the nomination to face Dewey in November. Veteran statewide campaigners such as Al Terrill and Charles Nesbitt expected to run well. However, former Congressman Ed Edmondson of Muskogee won the nomination, garnering almost 60 percent of the vote in the eleven-man field.

Oklahoma voters were given a clear choice in the 1972 Senate race. It was a choice not so much over issues, but over political philosophies. Dewey was a laid-back, easy-going conservative Republican. Edmondson was a fiery, aggressive liberal from a famous Oklahoma political family. *The Daily Oklahoman* summarized the differences when an editorial pointed out, "Bartlett is from Ohio, Ivy League, a Republican, a Catholic and a geologist who did not run for office until 10 years ago after he had achieved success in business. Edmondson has the easy manner with crowds and strangers you'd expect in a man who has been running for re-election every two years since 1948."

Consumer advocate Ralph Nader characterized Edmondson's philosophy as an "Oklahoma philosphy," a lot of emphasis on football, oil, and wide-open spaces. *The Daily Oklahoman,* in endorsing Dewey, said, "Even Bartlett's worst political enemies probably would not deny that he got into politics because he was moved by a genuine desire for public service." The newspaper called Edmondson, "the darling of Washington liberals."

The race went down to the wire. Newspapers reported that statewide polls showed the race a dead heat, even though most daily papers in the state endorsed Edmondson.

More than a million voters went to the polls on November 7. The Nixon-Agnew national ticket overwhelmed Democrats George McGovern and Sargeant Shriver in Oklahoma, piling up almost a three-to-one margin. The Republican landslide allowed Dewey to narrowly defeat Edmondson 516,934 to 478,212.

In his six years in the United States Senate Dewey exerted tremendous influence on behalf of his constituents in Oklahoma. He spoke out on every issue of the times. After returning from a trip to South Vietnam and Cambodia in early 1975, Dewey led the fight in the Senate for supplementary military assistance to South Vietnam and medical and food aid to Cambodia, "If either country falls because of inadequate ammunition, gasoline, medical or food supplies, our allies around the world will receive a message loud and clear. I am afraid that message will read that the U.S. has defaulted on its commitment to its friends. The dominoes that might tumble around the free world could be the confidence of friendly nations in the leadership ability of the U.S."

When South Vietnam and Cambodia fell to the Communists later that year, Dewey questioned how significant a role Congress should play in foreign affairs. He partially blamed the loss of the war on Congressional inaction, "Whether our national honor has been damaged might be subject to debate, but can anyone maintain that we have not lost credibility? Congressional vacillation, however well intended, has contributed to losses of prestige and credibility."

Dewey introduced a constitutional amendment for mandatory retirement of federal judges at age 70. He said, "It just makes no sense to allow persons executing the authority and responsibility of a federal judge to continue their duties at a time when they may not be fully capable either physically or mentally."

Dewey was a champion of the free-market system and a brilliant spokesman for America's oil and gas industry.

He did not hesitate to call federal power regulators on the carpet when he disagreed with their rulings. In 1975 the Federal Power Commission (FPC) limited the amount of natural gas available for agricultural irrigation. Dewey took personal privilege on the Senate floor, "Gambling with food production and the agricultural economy of this nation because of an ill-conceived ruling on natural gas usage warrants the determination, and yes, the courage, of the FPC to rescind that ruling."

In a letter to President Gerald Ford in 1976, Dewey cautioned against an immediate arms control agreement with the Soviet Union. He called the demands for haste "dangerous and unnecessary." In Dewey's opinion, "For the U.S., a bad treaty is worse than no treaty."

Dewey was one of the Senate's strongest proponents of the B-1 bomber program in 1976. He believed it was incumbent upon the Congress to support the program to

Dewey and Ann, 1960.

"signal clearly to the U.S.S.R. our resolve to remain number one in military preparedness."

By 1977 the abortion issue was a hotly-debated topic in Congress. There was no question on which side of the issue Dewey stood. He gave an impassioned speech in the Senate in June, 1977, in opposition to federal funding of discretionary abortions, "Albert Schweitzer long ago warned, 'If a man loses reverence for any part of life, he will lose his reverence for all life.' Public officials have dared to argue that it is cheaper for the federal government to abort a baby than to pay its mother additional welfare. How long will it take them to figure out how much cheaper it would be for Medicaid to hasten the death of the aged and infirm rather than support them in nursing homes?"

Dewey's training in the private business sector guided his opposition to big government and bureaucracy. He spoke against the Energy Act of 1978 and argued that the "bill is excessively burdensome. A massive regulatory bureaucracy is established to wreak havoc on utilities and industry and cost millions of taxpayer dollars in the process. This bureaucracy will ultimately publish thousands of pages of regulations and case records to monitor what would have happened anyway."

Dewey Bartlett was firmly entrenched in the Oklahoma and national political structure when he began having health problems in 1976. He was too tired too often. A checkup revealed a spot on his lung. The gloomy diagnosis was lung cancer, the same disease that had claimed the life of his brother David the year before. One of Dewey's first reactions to the news that he had cancer was that he did not have time to have cancer.

Most of 1977 was filled with chemotherapy and radiation therapy at Howard University in Washington, D.C. and at Sloan-Kettering Hospital in New York City. Even though he was weak Dewey managed to work an almost normal schedule in the Senate. Dewey and Ann struggled with the decision of whether or not to run for re-election in 1978. His health was deteriorating rapidly.

A meeting was called in January at the Bartlett home in Tulsa. Present were the Bartletts and their children, Mary Ann Freeman, Mike McCarville, Johnnie Cherblanc, Lee Rooker and others. There was open and frank discussion. Dewey was interested in everyone's opinion. Many urged him to run. Finally, Dewey said he did not think he could continue to serve in the Senate, run a campaign, and fight the cancer. The next morning he announced he would retire from the United States Senate and return home to Tulsa. Just before he walked into his office in Tulsa to face a sea of reporters, Dewey turned to McCarville and said, "Just help me do this gracefully."

Dewey did not give up easy. He left the Senate in October, 1978 and still thought he could win his battle with cancer. He and Ann took long walks and talked about things that he still wanted to do. He never felt short-changed by the cancer but still wanted to be of service to his neighbors as a college president or civic leader.

The dreaded cancer finally won and Dewey Bartlett left his beloved Oklahoma and his family on March 1, 1979, a few weeks before his sixtieth birthday. His life was over but his legacy will live forever in his adopted state.

SPEECHES OF
DEWEY F. BARTLETT

FROM THE
CONGRESSIONAL RECORD
AND THE
DEWEY F. BARTLETT COLLECTION
IN
THE ARCHIVES OF THE OKLAHOMA STATE LIBRARY

Wedding day, April 2, 1945, for Dewey and Ann at the famous mission at San Juan Capistrano, California.

CLASS PRESIDENT'S ADDRESS

May 1942, at Princeton University

Gentlemen of the Class of 1942:

Twenty-five years ago today, a class graduated from Princeton into a world torn by war. Tomorrow, we too graduate into a world torn by war. Like them, we will enter the service of our country, and I hope with the same unselfish spirit and patriotic enthusiasm. Like them, the outbreak of war has found us mentally unprepared to decide intelligently what our position should be in the war program. When war was declared in 1917, the romantic allure of excitement and adventure led undergraduates to abandon college life and join the armed forces. World War I revealed the grim realities and horrors of total war. Thus, in the few days after December 7, we were able to analyze the situation confronting us more maturely, and unemotionally, and decided that we could best serve the interests of our nation by completing the requirements for a college degree.

Within a short space of time, the University administration and officials in Washington confirmed the soundness of our decision—that of remaining in college to secure a degree. The position and problems of a University in time of war were discussed at length by the dean of the College and members of the Undergraduate Council. The ideas presented at this time were coordinated with those of the faculty and the government, and gave rise to the accelerated plan of study—the first well-rounded attempt by a University to gear itself to the demands of a country at war.

The relatively short space of time which remained in our college career lightened the burden of this choice. The underclasses and incoming freshmen are less fortunate.

Their choice of furthering their education is of necessity a long term proposition, and they may have misgivings as to the wiseness of remaining in college. They have friends who are already in uniform; they have friends who risk their lives every day on the far-flung battle fronts; and they have friends who have already given us their lives in one service or another. They realize that the patriotism and courage of remaining in college will have to withstand the criticism of unthinking and naive observers. They may feel that they could best serve their country by doing something direct, something measurable, something with physical relief. Not profiting by the experience of the first

(l to r) Mike, Dewey Jr., Dewey Sr., and Joanie in their backyard in Tulsa, 1952.

Joanie Bartlett

Dewey Bartlett, Jr.

World War, some of them may be attracted by the adventure and false glory of war. In their eagerness to participate in the war effort, they refuse to recognize the long term nature of our government's war program. They are thinking in terms of the present and immediate problem of winning the war quickly, and not of looking ahead at their part in the post-war peace.

The leaders of our country have clearly and repeatedly expressed their desire that all students remain in college to complete their education, and to obtain their degree. Undergraduates should realize that there is a well-trained selective service organization which will call upon them when they are needed. In addition, they can leave college at any time they so desire to join the armed forces. But if they are once in uniform and decide they could better serve their country by continuing their education, there is no road back, they have already lost the opportunity of returning to college.

A commission can not be substituted for a college degree. This was proven in the last war. Men who left college to join the Army or Navy found themselves inadequately prepared at the conclusion of hostilities to fill the jobs for which a college education would have fitted them.

The war has not only necessitated the adoption of the accelerated program, but it has also necessitated a change in the attitude of the student accepting the program. Princeton no longer has a place in its ranks for students who just get by, neither has it any place for those who continually belittle the value of a college education in our war effort. Princeton does want the student who approaches his obligations with stability of mind and sincerity of purpose. He should make every effort to attain the highest possible scholastic standing, and at the same time ready himself physically, as well as mentally, for the part he is to play in the service of his country, and the reorganization of the world to follow.

The problem of the undergraduate of tomorrow is to continue his college education, realizing that he has a dual purpose—to prepare himself more adequately for the immediate problem of the war, and also the future problem of the peace to follow. This is a definite challenge—a challenge that must be met.

INAUGURAL ADDRESS

On the south steps of the State Capitol, January 9, 1967

I appreciate the confidence you have shown in me. I want to tell each of you that I will do everything in my power to fulfill that confidence.

As I assume the important responsibilities of this office, I have an all too clear realization of my limitations. I doubt that any man could call himself truly prepared for this job.

I have sought, and will continue to seek, the guidance of Almighty God in the deliberations and decisions which will be mine in the coming months.

I thank Governor [Henry] Bellmon for his efforts toward making this change in administrations a smooth one. Along with a majority of Oklahomans, I am proud of the record he has made in the past four years. I am proud to be able to say that I was a member of his Legislative team.

He has served Oklahoma not only by being a good public official himself, but also by bringing to state government so many able public servants. Having these experienced people already on the job makes my work a great deal easier.

The Government of Oklahoma is a continuing institution and standing here on these historic steps, it is fitting that we remember the Governors and Legislative leaders of the past, living and dead, who have served this state. Each has made his contribution to our heritage.

Compared to the other states, our history is short. We are young. Our generation of Oklahomans is vigorous and hungry for progress. Our young people are proud of their state and of themselves. They have a self assurance equaled only by the first residents of this State. Our young people want to stay in Oklahoma and they will if we can provide the jobs they seek. Our young people want their future in Oklahoma. Our future is in our young people.

We realize the problems in both rural and urban areas of the State are caused by a rapid migration from the farms to the cities and towns. The citizens of the two metropolitan areas, and the rapidly growing cities and towns must recognize their responsibilities in developing the economy of the rural areas.

Those in the rural areas must be concerned with urban problems and assist in their solution.

But though we have different problems, we are not two different peoples. We are one. We are Oklahomans. Together we have come through good times and bad and we are no longer afraid of change.

We are a wealthy State. Our wealth lies in our People -- strong people of pioneer and Indian stock. People from all parts of the country and beyond. People who have overcome the difficulties of the past. People who are ready and willing to face the future.

The government of Oklahoma in the next four years will stand shoulder to shoulder with all of you in pursuing our dreams for that future. Of course, government is not productive in the way that factories and farms are productive. In fact, it is just the opposite. For it is a burden on the productive capacities of our people. But government has a part to play in progress.

It is the duty of government to provide the arena in which every citizen may freely advance to the limits of his ability...peacefully and in harmony with his fellow citizens. And it is the duty of government to provide this arena economically.

There is today a rising tide of confidence in Oklahoma government. It is easy to see the results of this confidence. Recent administrations have returned numerous functions of government to the local level. And local citizens have taken up that challenge, providing for themselves when they were shown the need. This is the highest vote of confidence any state government could receive.

Yes, the climate is improving, but there is much left to accomplish....more than we shall manage in one Legislative session. But now there is a will to get on with the job! To do this, the chief executive and the legislature must work together. The Legislative leaders, and I as your Governor, have pledged our mutual cooperation.

We are going to use all of our talents and abilities. We are going to experiment and innovate. We are going to recognize our mistakes and correct them.

In the Executive Department there is a need for greater efficiency. We must continue to improve the efficiency of government. We shall work together to make these improvements. Of course, we shall remember the old cattleman's rule: "Never take a fence down until you know why it was put up." So we shall examine our fences carefully. We shall find out why they were put up. And when we find a fence that has outlived its usefulness, we will take it down, saving the posts and wire where possible...in the interests of economy.

By your votes you have given me the ultimate challenge...the challenge of leadership. I accept it. But I also have a challenge for you. Wherever you are, look around you. Look at your job, your home, yourself, your community, your state. I challenge you to set a new standard of excellence for yourself. Hold to that standard out of your pride in being an Oklahoman.

This has been a sobering occasion for me. But it has also been an occasion of excitement...excitement which I feel for the future of Oklahoma. You feel that same excitement...you have told me so in hundreds of visits in every part of the State.

From that excitement will come a great future for us

all. I ask each of you to join me now to bring our future to reality.

Dewey Bartlett and Administrative Assistant Robert Herring, 1966.

OKIES ALL

A speech to unveil the OKIE program, May 2, 1968

There once was a time, not so long ago, when, if you called someone an Okie, you had better be pretty big or a good runner.

An effort is being made to change that, and the effort so far has been quite successful. This effort to stir pride in Oklahoma involves turning that Dust Bowl epithet into a modern day theme.

The OKIE program has attracted nationwide attention.

We have redefined OKIE to mean "Oklahoma, Key to Industrial Expansion," "Oklahoma, Key to Individual Enthusiasm," and "Oklahoma, Key to Intelligence and Enterprise."

We're all proud of Oklahoma, so we ought to know some facts about the State that allows us to translate our pride to others.

I have an incomplete list of famous Okies. I'd like to read it to you. It is an example of what we have to offer as a State, and it shows very plainly that we've got a lot of which to be proud.

Mickey Mantle, Warren Spahn, Carl Hubbell, Dizzy and Paul Dean, Allie Reynolds, Pepper Martin, Paul and Lloyd Waner, Tom Sturdivant, Cal McLish, Dom Demeter, Alvin Dark, and Ralph Terry.

Those are the athletes. Here are some others:

Jayne Jayroe, Miss America of 1967, from Laverne; Debi Faubion, from Norman, was the 1967 Miss Teenage America. Gretchen Wyler, from Bartlesville, is an internationally-acclaimed actress. Norma Smallwood, Miss America of 1927, was a Tulsan.

Among Oklahoma's other famed sons and daughters are Jim G. Lucas, a Muskogee and Tulsa newspaperman who went on to win the Pulitzer Prize and the Ernie Pyle Award for excellence in news reporting. The 1967 co-winner of the Ernie Pyle Award was Bill Thomas, a former Oklahoma City newspaperman.

Paul Harvey is a native Okie, as is Paul Hood, senior editor of the *National Observer.* Douglas Edwards is an Ada boy and Frank McGee grew up in Oklahoma City.

Will Rogers, the greatest home-spun humorist who ever lived, was an Okie. Wiley Post, world-famous aviator and Will Rogers' companion, also was an Okie.

Thomas P. Stafford and LeRoy Gordon Cooper, members of America's astronaut team are Okies. Tom Stafford is one of the proudest Okies we've got, and you'll be hearing more about that.

Jim Thorpe, the greatest athlete who ever lived, was an Oklahoma Indian.

Oklahoma has 63 Indian tribes, by latest count, which is more tribes than any other state. For almost 100 years before Statehood in 1907, the Five Civilized Tribes — Chickasaw, Cherokee, Choctaw, Seminole and Creek — maintained separate governments of their own. Their proud heritage is cherished by today's Oklahomans.

Sequoyah, an Oklahoma Indian Chief, invented the Cherokee alphabet. P. K. Wrigley invented chewing gum at Guthrie, Oklahoma. The first parking meter in the world was developed by Professor H.G. Thuesen and G.A. Hale of Oklahoma State University, and Carl C. McGee, and installed in Oklahoma City in 1935, which is testimony to the inventiveness of Oklahoma's citizens.

General Stand Watie, an Oklahoma Indian, was the last confederate General to surrender to the Union, a distinction which testified to the depth of his commitment to his loyalties.

Jim Shoulders, world champion cowboy, hails from Henryetta, Oklahoma.

S.N. Goldman, an Oklahoman, invented the rolling supermarket basket.

Bill Pickett was an Oklahoma Negro, a cowboy at the famous 101 Ranch, and he is credited with having invented the art of bull-dogging, or steer-wrestling.

The famous spiritual, "Swing Low Sweet Chariot" was composed by two Negro slaves, Uncle Wallace Willis and Aunt Minerva Willis, his wife, and they also wrote "Steal Away to Jesus" and "I'm a Rollin'."

Lynn Riggs of Claremore, another great Okie, wrote the play "Oklahoma," which produced Oklahoma's State song and spread Oklahoma's glories around the world through song.

Paul Miller, president of the Gannett newspapers, is an Oklahoman, as is Allan Cromley, past president of the National Press Club in Washington.

Larry Gaffnew, Director of Public Information for the United States Information Agency, is an Okie. Harold Keith of Norman is a nationally-recognized author of fiction for young adults, and recently was named one of America's outstanding authors. Jack Bickham, also of Norman has written 24 novels and is being acclaimed as one of America's emerging young novelists. Admiral George M. Davis of Bixby is Surgeon General of the Navy. General William Garrison of Oklahoma City is retired Inspector General for the entire United States Army.

Jane Mayo, an Okie, was a world's champion all-around cowgirl. Jerri Cobb, another Okie, was named "Aviation Woman of 1959," and was the first American woman to pass tests for astronautical training. She also captured from the Soviet Union the world's speed record for light twin-engine aircraft in an Aero Commander, manufactured in Oklahoma.

Tulsa is the home of the National Headquarters of the Junior Chamber of Commerce, and the Society for the

Preservation and Encouragement of Barbershop Quartet Singing in America was founded in Tulsa and Tulsa is now that organization's national headquarters.

Robert L. Owens, the first United States Senator from Oklahoma, authored the law creating the Federal Reserve Bank System and he also was the first Okie ever to be balloted on as a nominee for President of the United States. Oklahoma produced and elected the first woman member of Congress to preside over that great body. She was Alice Robertson, a Republican, from Muskogee.

James Garner, G.D. Spradlin, Dale Robertson, Patti Page, Molly Bee, Jennifer Jones, Kay Starr, Clu Galager, Anita Bryant, Robert Reed, Van Heflin, Dennis Weaver and other actors and actresses are Okies.

America's leading ballerinas, including Marie Tallchief, Yvonne Chouteau, Rosella Hightower and Moscelyne Larkin, are Oklahomans.

Mrs. Betty Cole Dukert, associate producer of "Meet the Press," is a native Okie.

Dick Rowan, of Rowan and Martin, hails from Beggs.

And here's a list of other Okies whose achievements set them apart:

Jimmy Ling, president of Ling-Temco-Vought; Deacon New of Oklahoma City, past national president of the Petroleum Writers of America; Harry Culver of Oklahoma City, past president of the National Wire Service guild; Stella Roberts, Oklahoma City, past secretary-treasurer of the National Wire Service guild; Ralph Sewell of Oklahoma City, past national president of Sigma Delta Chi, professional journalism society; Bruce Palmer, of Oklahoma City, past national president, Radio-TV News Director's Association; Ed Stanley, past national president of the Association of Newspaper Classified Advertising Managers, Inc.; Miss Edna Donley, former National Teacher of the Year; Mrs. Lawana Trout, 1964 National Teacher of the Year; Dr.

Chesley Martin, named National Family Doctor of the year by the American Medical Association; and Mrs. E. Lee Ozbirn, past international president of the federation of Women's Clubs.

There are more:

Herb Karner of Tulsa, past president of the Farm Editors of America; Eddie Miller of Mangum, who wrote "Release Me," the all-time best seller in country and western music; J.C. Cobb, past president of the National Association of Retail Druggists; Patrick J. Hurley, a member of President Hoover's Cabinet; Judge Juanita Kidd Stout, the first elected Negro judge in Philadelphia; Gordon W. Lillie, or Pawnee Bill, known for his historic Wild West shows; Lee Hazelwood of Mannford, whose songs have made Nancy Sinatra a leading singer; Woody Guthrie, the late folk song master; Bobby Ussery of Morris, a jockey who won the Kentucky Derby; Miss Malinda Berry, former America's Maid of Cotton; Miss Sandra Sue Stout, former National Dairy Princess and Samuel G. Chapman of Norman, former staff member of the President's Crime Commission. In politics, there's U.S. Senator Fred Harris and James Jones; Bryce Harlow and Bud Wilkinson, Carl Albert; and you can probably think of some I haven't mentioned.

As you can see, the influence of Oklahoma's sons and daughters has spread far beyond the borders of the State. Their accomplishments are many and as their reputations spread, so does our pride in them.

I would like also to give you some general, but not too well-known, facts about Oklahoma.

Oklahoma has been under 14 flags in her recorded years of history.

Oklahoma had the first flowing commercial oil well in the world.

Oklahoma is the International Home of the Rainbow Girls.

Oklahoma has the largest Scottish Rite Temple in the world.

The first Boy Scout Troop in America was formed in Oklahoma in 1909 by the Reverend John F. Mitchel.

Oklahoma is the home of the National Cowboy Hall of Fame and Western Heritage Center.

Oklahoma is winter quarters for more circuses than any other State.

Oklahoma has more shoreline than the Atlantic Coast.

I want to conclude by pointing out what is perhaps the most interesting of all these facts, and that is that the word OKIE has been traced by the Governor's office to 1907, the year of Oklahoma Statehood and more than 30 years before Steinbeck wrote his *Grapes of Wrath*.

Significantly, the original meaning of the word was, "One from Oklahoma." Even in the early depression days, the word was used to describe hard-working individuals temporarily out of work but nonetheless trying to provide for their families.

Unfortunately, it was Steinbeck's version of Okie that got all the publicity, despite the fact that version was a fictionalized inaccuracy.

The publicity now is going to the new OKIE, however, and the word has become a rallying point for those involved in stimulating Oklahoma's industrial and economic growth, its tourism potential and its proud record of accomplishment.

I hope you will join in the effort to create pride in Oklahoma through the OKIE program.

RICHARD NIXON IS MY CHOICE

At the 1968 Republican National Convention

I am withdrawing as a favorite son candidate for the Republican nomination for the Office of President of the United States.

I thank the Oklahoma delegation for its support. To those Oklahomans who worked on my nominating speeches — Congressman Jim Smith, Tulsa County Republican Chairman Ed Lawson, Attorney General G.T. Blankenship and House Minority Leader Jim Connor — my special thanks.

I have refrained during this campaign from making public my personal choice for the nomination. I wanted a hard-hitting but positive campaign on the issues, which I believe we have had.

I authored the Jackson Hole, Wyoming Resolution which favored uninstructed delegations to this convention. The man I support for the nomination has supported uninstructed delegations and did so before and after the Jackson Hole Resolution, clearly displaying his desire for an open campaign to allow every candidate to freely present his credentials to the people.

He stands out for his persistent interest in Oklahoma. He has visited Oklahoma frequently, over a period of years, and has shared with our citizens the beauty of our many lakes and our forests and park areas. He knows the real Oklahoma, and he knows it is a growing, beautiful state.

He has seen the eager faces of Oklahoma's willing labor force, a force that provides business and industry with the finest employees available anywhere. He has seen the modern skylines of Oklahoma City and Tulsa and he is familiar with Oklahoma's agricultural achievements and needs.

He has consistently encouraged the use of private enterprise to provide more and better jobs, as I have, and he stands as a strong advocate of a workable, equitable state-federal relationship. He has identified an overriding strategic need in America and that is to lure industry into rural areas to reverse the flow of rural poor to the cities. He is devoted to bringing human dignity to each American.

Dewey, Richard Nixon, and Henry Bellmon, 1963.

He has by his past actions proven himself a man of ability, integrity, character and resolve. He has by his past actions shown himself to be an able politician, a willing co-worker, a man who has put party ahead of self and nation ahead of party.

He has spoken out strongly, and eloquently, on the problem of crime in America and how we should begin to solve it. He believes that spending more money than is available constitutes fiscal irresponsibility.

Though this loyal American knows Oklahoma and Oklahomans, the important qualification he possesses is that he knows each state, and its citizens—he knows America and Americans. His knowledge of America is matched by his experience and competency in foreign affairs.

He has offered constructive, decisive criticisms, and he has offered constructive, decisive solutions. His criticisms have been responsible and well-reasoned, and I am confident he will carry with him to the White House the same intelligent, rational approach to the serious and nagging problems which now confront all America.

I want a winner, and I endorse Richard Nixon as the man who will win now, who will win in November, and who will win for every American for the next four years.

Dewey as a United States Senator in his Capitol Hill office, 1974.

Dewey's 1966 Campaign brochure.

WILL ROGERS WOULD HAVE LIKED THE OKIE PROGRAM

A speech at Claremore, Oklahoma, November 4, 1968

We are here today to honor the memory of Will Rogers, an original Okie who carried the story of Oklahoma's warmth and vitality all across the nation. I want to tell you of the reception our OKIE program has received across the country.

As you may know, we kicked off the OKIE program last May. We apply OKIE to mean, Oklahoma, Key to Industrial Expansion and Oklahoma, Key to Intelligence and Enterprise.

We have sought to turn an apology into an asset, and we believe the effort is paying dividends. This is consistent with Will Rogers' approach to life.

We have a two-drawer file cabinet which is filled with letters from hundreds of Okies, past and present, saluting this effort to promote pride in Oklahoma. We receive an average of five letters a day from individuals who want OKIE pins or OKIE certificates.

Earlier this week, we received a letter from a teacher in the Panhandle. Using the OKIE program, she had asked her students to prepare short "Pride in Oklahoma" essays. They did so, and requested OKIE pins for the writers of the best essays.

We received a letter from a woman in California who left Oklahoma during the dust bowl days. She wrote to thank me for our attempts to bring honor to a word she once was ashamed to hear. She now wears an OKIE pin, as do her four children.

From Thomas came this letter: "We have our OKIE certificates framed for all to see and we are proud of them."

From a Pawnee native in Big Bend National Park, Texas: "It has come to my attention that you have available a document known as the OKIE Certificate. I understand this certificate is directed toward education of the uninformed, information for the unenlightened, and a direct rebuttal of the slur frequently associated with the term OKIE. It's about time! Good for you! I would be very proud to have one to frame and display."

From Tulsa: "How can I obtain an OKIE pin? All Okies should be proud to wear one."

From New York: "I am deeply grateful for the great honor which the wonderful state of Oklahoma has conferred upon me."

From White Plains, NY: "Let me say it's okay to be an Okie."

From Texhoma: "I wish to congratulate you on your idea of the OKIE program. I think this is a very clever idea in order to create a pride in Oklahomans in the history and progress of our state and also offset the trend in other states to make fun of Okies. Thank you very much for the recognition, and the development of pride in Oklahoma."

From El Reno: "Having been associated with the administration of Governor Leon Phillips at the time John Steinbeck wrote his best selling book and thereby inspired the bitter resentment of Governor Phillips, I am happy to have lived through the period during which the implication of the name Okie has completely reversed itself. You are responsible in a great measure for this."

VETERANS DAY REMARKS

Presented at Shidler, Oklahoma, November 11, 1968

Today, we pause to honor those millions of Americans whose gallantry, courage, sacrifice and compassion have protected our shores and our homes and the homes of others for the years of our national independence.

Throughout the conflicts that have wracked the world, American fighting men have written chapters of bravery and dedication that light the way for the other nations of the world.

It was the sacrifices and courage of the American veteran that allowed America to be born, to grow and to keep growing.

America is strong today because its fighting men inherited from their fathers and forefathers the same fighting spirit that causes us to honor all veterans here this morning.

Today is also the 50th anniversary of the end of the great war — World War I. On this historic day 50 years ago, the first of more than 26 million Americans to serve since that time put up their weapons and came marching home.

We know that those veterans, more than anyone, hate war. We know that none of us are more dedicated to peace, and we know that because our veterans have seen the horror of war, they know we must communicate to the world our unending desire for peace and progress.

On this Veteran's Day, 1968, we salute the willingness of ordinary Americans to give their lives for their country, and in memory of those who have gone ahead of us in service to their country, we should rededicate ourselves to the pursuit of peace.

In my proclamation setting today aside as Veterans Day, I urged all Oklahomans to support their fighting men and to honor their veterans.

It is fitting that today we are gathered here to do just that, and I salute all of you for your love of country, love of state and love for your fellow man.

I also want to tell you that our veterans who are fighting today in Vietnam have a great pride in their country, and in Oklahoma. Once or twice a week, I receive a request for an Oklahoma flag to fly over an outpost in Vietnam, or to be mounted on the lead vehicle of an Oklahoma unit.

The thank-you letters I receive are eloquent testimony to the reasons for our presence here: the letters speak of a desire to protect the freedom-loving peoples of the world, and to bring peace to them and to their children. They speak also of a thankfulness that the ferocity of war has not visited Oklahoma, and that their wives and their children are safe at home today.

They tell us that war is hell and men die, but freedom has its price. They are proud to be called veterans and those who were veterans before them now benefit from their special understanding of the man who has defended his country with rifle and bayonet, ship or airplane.

We honor all our veterans, especially those serving today. Our hearts go out to them, and to their families, and especially on this day, we pray that future days will see them home safe once again.

To those who fall, and to those who have fallen, we recognize a special responsibility. That responsibility is to always cherish what they fought to preserve, and to guard, as they did, America's great heritage and tremendous future.

THE OKIE WAY

A speech to the Oklahoma City Chamber of Commerce,
July 15, 1969

Ladies and gentlemen, this will be an ear-bender.

For the next 30 minutes, I am going to let loose one continuous stream of unmitigated truth about the greatest state in the Union--Oklahoma--and about the efforts of its leaders to rejuvenate its rural areas, to pump new life into its economy, and to bring new Okies in and old Okies back.

The title of this speech is "The OKIE Way", and I'd like to explain what that means. More than a year ago, I, and others, sensed that a dramatic and continuing public relations program to stir pride in Oklahoma was needed. We began with a "Pride in Oklahoma" campaign, complete with advertising and bumper stalkless. Led by *The Daily Oklahoman* in Oklahoma City with the cooperation of other news media, the campaign stressed how far our state had come in just 60 years of statehood. We then took the worst connotation of our state we could think of, and that was John Steinbeck's portrayal of what he believed to be the Oklahomans of the 1930's. The derogatory title of Okie, as applied to Steinbeck's fictional characters, had hung over Oklahoma for 30 years. We didn't like it. We didn't like it worth a hoot!

So we took the name OKIE, and applied it to Oklahoma today, in 1968. We applied the initials in this way: O for Oklahoma, K for key, I for intelligence, and E for enterprise, which I believe typifies today's Oklahoman. And because of our need for industrial development, we applied the initials even further and came up with O for Oklahoma, K for key, I for industrial and E for expansion, which gave us two mottos: Oklahoma, Key to Intelligence and Enterprise and Oklahoma, Key to Industrial Expansion.

The gold pin in my lapel reads Okie. In the O is a drop of water representing Oklahoma's 1,500 square miles of inland water. Among the states, Oklahoma ranks 10th in the amount of water and probably first in the amount of water available to industry and municipalities. In the I is an evergreen tree, representing Oklahoma's 75,000 acres of green forests and rolling prairies, its 14 special recreation areas and 21 state parks, including 7 lodges.

The Okie program is meant to represent today's Oklahoma--a state filled with aggressive, willing to work and well-educated individuals who offer a day's work for a day's pay. It is meant to stir pride in Oklahoma and to promote our industrial effort.

Since my inauguration in January of 1967, Oklahoma's industrial development program has been my prime concern. I was elected on my pledge that I'd be Oklahoma's job-gettingest governor. I had plenty of skeptics, too. Some thought I was whistling Dixie with an Oklahoma tune. But by now many of you have heard of our industry-seeking efforts, and that's why I'm here, to tell you about it in detail and with vigor, and I intend to do just that.

I'd like to preface Oklahoma's industrial story by citing a problem. In the five-year period beginning in 1960, the federal, state and local governments spent $5 billion in Oklahoma in on-going education, highway, mental health and welfare programs. At the beginning of that five year period, Oklahoma lagged $380 behind the national average in per capita income. After spending $5 billion, the per capita income gap 5 years later stood at nearly $600 behind the national average.

Obviously, the government's efforts have not done the

job. In recent years, Oklahoma's per capita income ranking has climbed from 40th to 36th. Haves have more--the have nots have less. Raising the per capita income to the national average would have raised Oklahoma's tax take by $350 million, or an average of $70 million a year. That's the equivalent of a two-cent sales tax increase, or more than a doubling of the individual and corporate income tax, or doubling the gasoline and fuels excise tax.

We recognize that only nine per cent of Oklahoma's jobs outside the metropolitan areas are in manufacturing. With shrinking labor requirements in both agriculture and petroleum, there is an imperative need that Oklahoma succeed in attracting new industry. And we are succeeding.

We recognize that Oklahoma must move to close the income gap. To close the gap, we openly and unashamedly court many of America's leading companies. In 18 months, I have personally called on the officers of 80 of America's largest 500 companies and 20 of the top 50 com-

On the campaign trail in 1965 with Ralph Thompson and G.T. Blankenship.

panies, as well as many smaller companies. When we began this program, I initiated what I call the "one a day brand" method of personal contact. This has grown to two or three telephone calls a day to out-of-state industrial leaders to tell them what Oklahoma has to offer. I point out the profit climate in Oklahoma and what we are doing to help our present industry, because how we help them affects our image with new industry.

Senator Bartlett surrounded by his pages, 1966.

TAX REFORM

A speech to the Oklahoma Press Association,
January 23, 1970

It's always a pleasure to be with newsmen! That's true because I was talking with Vice President [Spiro] Agnew and he assured me I'd enjoy it, particularly if the networks are represented.

The recent pleas for "tax reform" in Oklahoma remind me of the young man who, after being sentenced to hang, was asked by the judge if he had anything to say. "But Judge," said the young man, "I can't stand to be hanged." The Judge thoughtfully replies: "Well, stand as much of it as you can."

In my opinion the taxpayers of Oklahoma have stood about all the so-called "tax reforms" they can. The furor for tax reform began in late December when the President Pro-Tempore of the Senate wrote me suggesting we put aside partisan politics (join hands, so-to-speak) and make tax reform in Oklahoma a reality. Then, Mr. J.C. Kennedy, Chairman of the Democratic party in Oklahoma, issued a news release supporting Senator [Finis] Smith. To his letter Senator Smith attached a list of so-called "fat cat deductions" and existing "loopholes" in the present law which he said (and I have no reason to doubt him) would increase state revenue by approximately $100 million dollars. It is amazing to me that this request for $100 million dollar tax increase on Oklahoma citizens did not list the purposes for which the tax increase would be spent, and comes at a time when tax collections are at an all-time high and in a year of the largest legal increase in general revenue funds in the history of Oklahoma.

His fact sheet contained five illustrations of the type of tax reform proposals he advocated:

1. Repeal of the exemption of domestic insurance companies from the 4% premium tax paid by foreign insurance companies.

2. Elimination of non-taxable corporate dividends.

3. Repeal of sales tax exemptions.

4. Restoration of the 1947 income tax "cuts" to corporations and

5. Elimination of deductions for federal income tax payments on state income tax returns.

I replied to his letter and declined his invitation to sponsor his proposals, because I believe they constitute a general tax increase, rather than tax reform.

Early this month, Senator Smith wrote me a second letter. He expressed surprise at my opposition to his program for tax reform and requested that I keep an open mind on the subject. He also expressed his intention to create a special committee, composed of six members to be appointed by the legislature and three members to be appointed by me to study his proposal for tax reform. Mr. Kennedy endorsed this plan also. In reply to the second letter, I referred Senator Smith to my previous letter which I felt adequately stated my position on his proposals. I offered to meet with him personally to discuss the matter further if he deemed such a meeting necessary. To date, he has not requested such a meeting.

At the outset, let me make three general statements regarding my position on this matter.

1. I am not opposed to tax reform. I am opposed to a tax increase disguised as, and labeled tax reform.

Specifically, I am opposed, for the reasons I will state later, to the proposals of Senator Smith.

2. The substantive provisions of the present tax laws were, almost without exception, enacted by democratic legislatures under the leadership of democratic governors. I cannot and will not defend any true "loopholes" or "inequities" which may exist in these laws, or any others. Let those who are responsible for their enactment, defend their validity.

3. True tax reform takes time. It cannot be accomplished in a few months.

Ideally, the tax structure of a state should be designed to accomplish certain things:

1. The tax laws should be written to provide sufficient revenue to finance the necessary functions of government.

2. The tax burden should be equitably and fairly distributed so that each taxpayer pays no more than his fair share of taxes.

3. The method of paying taxes should be as simple as possible; and,

4. The laws should be administered fairly, firmly and impartially, any proposal for tax reform should be directed toward the accomplishment of these purposes.

The term tax reform means different things to different persons.

To some, it means a tax increase.

To others, it means a tax reduction.

Still others consider it a tax directed at someone else.

To me, it has a different meaning.

To me, true tax reform means to change existing laws in such a manner as to accomplish either:

1. A more equitable distribution of the tax burden, or

2. A simpler method of paying taxes, or

3. A more efficient and fair method of tax collection.

Without at the same time increasing the overall tax burden. This may mean increased taxes for some, but it also means decreases for others.

For example, if Uncle John has an income of $10,000 and pays $500 in taxes while Aunt Minnie who has an equal amount of income and dependents pays $1,000 in taxes, my interpretation of the term "tax reform" would mean that we increase John's taxes by $250 but at the same time we reduce Minnie's taxes by $250. Each would, after tax reform, pay an equal amount of tax. The state would, after tax reform, derive an equal amount of revenue.

If, in this example, we merely increase John's taxes to $1,000, where is the "tax reform?" What relief have we given Minnie? Have we not merely increased John's taxes under the guise of reform?

If we examine Senator Smith's proposals in the light of my interpretation of tax reform, it becomes readily apparent why I oppose his program.

His first proposal - to repeal the exemption of domestic insurance companies from the 4% premium tax paid by foreign insurance companies--constitutes nothing more than a tax increase on domestic insurance companies. This exemption was supported by Governor [Robert S.] Kerr to strengthen and enlarge Oklahoma's domestic insurance industry.

His second proposal--to eliminate non-taxable corporate

dividends--constitutes a tax increase on every individual Oklahoma taxpayer who owns stock in any domestic corporation including any taxpayer having an account in an Oklahoma savings and loan association.

His third proposal--to repeal the sales tax exemptions - constitutes a tax increase on every manufacturer, every farmer, every dues-paying member of any fraternal, religious, civic, charitable or educational organization, every church, every purchaser of school lunches, every purchaser of a motor vehicle, every advertiser, every wholesaler, every retailer, every city, every town, and every county. In short, on every Oklahoman.

Parenthetically, since most of you are familiar with the sales tax exemption on advertising--let me ask you a question. If the sales tax exemption on advertising is removed will you not simply pass this along to the merchants in your home town? Won't they in turn pass it on to the consuming public? Does this not then constitute a general tax increase on the public?

Dewey and Ann with Mayor and Mrs. James M. Hewgley, Jr. at a dinner honoring the Gilcrease Museum in Tulsa, 1967.

His fourth proposal--to restore the 1947 income tax cut to corporations--is an out-and-out, clear-cut, tax increase on corporations.

His fifth proposal--to eliminate the deduction for federal income tax payments on state income tax returns--is a tax increase on every Oklahoman who pays income taxes.

Where is there reform in any of these measures? Where is there relief for any over-burdened taxpayer? Where is the relief for any of you? The proposals are simply a tax increase under the guise of tax reform.

Let me reiterate. I do not necessarily defend any of the above exemptions. At the same time, I do not condemn all of them as being "unfair" or "loopholes." I simply point out--in as clean language as possible--that what has been proposed is a general tax increase--one way or another--upon every taxpayer of this state.

In his second letter, Senator Smith stated his intention to seek legislative authority to create a special committee, composed of six members to be appointed by the legislature and three members to be appointed by me to study his proposals.

If such a committee is created by the legislature, I will appoint members to the committee as directed by the legislature. I always attempt to honor any legislative directive.

However, the proposal for membership on this committee is patently politically-inspired.

The constitution establishes the executive and legislative branches of government as co-equals. The proposal of Senator Smith fails to recognize this constitutional concept. He equates the House of Representatives with the executive and he equates the Senate with the executive, giving to the legislature a 6-3 majority on the committee. This violates the constitutional concept of separate but co-equal branches of government.

In my opinion, this constitutional concept requires that such a committee as Senator Smith proposes be composed of an equal number of members appointed by the legislature and by the executive.

As I said, I am not opposed to tax reform provided it is designed to accomplish one or preferably all of the purposes which I previously outlined and provided it meets my definition of tax reform.

My record on tax reform speaks for itself. As a member of the Senate, I supported legislation to make public the names of individuals and corporations filing or failing to file income tax returns. I was a member of the 1964/3-5 interim committee which thoroughly studied and recodified the existing tax laws. These are true tax reforms.

As Governor, I have, among other things, advocated legislation to upgrade the Office of County Assessor, to bring about equalization of ad valorem taxes and to simplify the filing of state income tax returns. In addition, I have encouraged the Oklahoma Tax Commission in its efforts to administer the tax laws fairly, firmly, and impartially, these again, are true "tax reforms."

I will, as Governor, or as a private citizen, continue to support any real--any bona fide--any non-partisan--effort to accomplish tax reform.

But true tax reform can only be accomplished under certain conditions:

1. There must be adequate study of all existing tax laws to determine upon whom the burden of taxes now falls.

2. Any proposed changes should be adopted only after those affected are afforded an opportunity to appear and be heard on the proposal.

3. Politics should in no way influence the decision to

recommend or fail to recommend any proposed change.

These conditions do not exist now.

There has not been an adequate study of all our tax laws. The atmosphere of "politics" completely dominates the capitol today. True tax reform cannot and will not be accomplished this highly political year. The pleas for tax reform will, like the windmill, continue to rotate but go nowhere.

This is not to say, however, that true tax reform can never be accomplished. It can--and it should be. I am willing to work toward that end.

To the advocates of tax reform, I issue this dual challenge! If you are sincere in your plea for tax reform, let's get on with the task in an orderly manner! Let us create a committee composed of an equal number of members appointed by the executive and by the legislative to study our present tax law--not now--not in the political atmosphere prevailing at the state capitol, but during the legislative interim as all other such important matters are studied. Let us consider tax decreases where warranted. Let us appropriate funds for immediate--competent--non-partisan --expert research. Let us attempt to equalize--not increase -- the tax burden.

If you are not sincere in your plea for true tax reform--if what you seek is a tax increase rather than tax reform--then get on with it! You have adequate votes to accomplish your objective. You do not need my support nor my leadership. You have the power, — but you have no right --to accomplish your purpose under the guise of tax reform!

GOVERNOR'S PRAYER BREAKFAST

April 6, 1970

Whenever two or more persons get together to unite in prayer, they attest to the fact that there is between them a uniting common bond. This is a bond on a spiritual plane above and beyond them, and not of their making, to which each of them may appeal and to which each of them must respond. They thus become witnesses, individually, and collectively and-mutually, to the common religious nature of all men, and to the existence and presence of God in their lives. In addition to, recognizing a common bond, a prayer uttered implies a purpose, a need and the expectation of a response. These are the simplest laments of prayer, and they are the basis for our dependence upon it.

Men uniting in prayer affirm a great principle, that is the foundation of the Hebraic and Christian faiths and this is the Principle of Divine Law. When translated into Morals and Ethics, it is the principle that the concept of Right and of Wrong, and of Good and of Bad are not left entirely to the sole discretion of any individual, but that such concepts arise from qualities implicit in man's nature and in God's order of things and events. When translated into Law these concepts become the things and acts designated in the democratic process as Licit and Illicit, constituting the legal limitations and boundaries of our acts, which we must observe until such designations are changed by the same process through which they came into force.

Flowing from this principle are corollary principles which undergird our idea of objective law, not of individual man's making, but of eternal divine creation, to which all men everywhere are subject. All must obey it, all may enjoy its benefits and all must suffer its penalties if it is violated. Men cannot be united in prayer until they are willing to submit to such a higher order, which measures them, compels them, restrains them and responds to them.

Yet, when two or more men unite in prayer, they each remain an individual spiritual character. If there is one function that no man can do for another, it is TO BELIEVE. This forms the unique individuality of men because the mind and spirit of one can never be the mind and spirit of another. This is the uniqueness of personality. EVERY PERSON IS A PERSON.

It was within the framework of this philosophy that provisions were written into our State Constitution and into the Federal Constitution guaranteeing, the right of freedom of religion and the separation of church and state--provisions which I, as Governor, am sworn to uphold and which you, as citizens, are bound to observe. The makers of our National Constitution learned from history and actual experience that individuals could not be compelled to believe alike in religion. But they could believe alike and agree on a united form of government to insure this right of individual religious belief. In the formation of our national union the people would not accept the unity in government until they were assured that it would restate and affirm the diversity in religion. People would not unite in their ideas of government until they were assured it would preserve their differences in religion. Men were able to forget their diverse ideas of government in order for government to guarantee and preserve to each of them their individually different religious sentiments. THIS IS ONE OF THE GREATEST PRACTICAL CONTRIBUTIONS AMERICANS HAVE MADE IN THE ENTIRE HISTORY OF POLITICAL SCIENCE. Guaranteeing to each individual his right to his religious belief was written into our basic law not because religion was unimportant, but because it was of paramount importance.

The separation of church and state in our fundamental law did not declare nor does it require a separation of citizen and God; in fact, it was written there to make way for people to have and maintain their own unfettered relationship with God.

When we join here to unite in a prayer service, we reaffirm both principles--separation of government and religion, and the unity of religious truth that each of us must observe.

The words of the *Lords Prayer* and of the *Psalmist's* songs proclaim the power of God, His presence, and how we should approach Him, and these point the way for us.

We should BELIEVE FIRMLY, ACT FAITHFULLY, and PRAY FRUITFULLY. These three are intertwined.

If we believe firmly and know what we believe, we can

Mike and Joanie Bartlett, 1960.

find direction and purpose in life and in living.

If we act faithfully we will sort out the waste and arrive at considered conclusions; thus be true to ourselves and our fellow man and faithful to God's purposes.

If we pray fruitfully, we will help bring into being what we pray for, and be prepared for the wholesome fruition of our aspiration. If a man prays and is not prepared for the answer to it, he may never know that it was answered. If a man prays for action and is not prepared to act, he has done a vain and profane thing. If a person prays for contentment in his spirit, how can he accept spiritual contentment if he is unhappy, upset and indifferent to the quality of life he asked for. If a man prays for courage and then runs from every task requiring a decision, how can he be courageous. So, when we pray, let us be prepared to accept the fruits of our prayer.

In summary, let our prayers here today express the individual spiritual aspirations of each of us, but let us recognize the overriding power of God under whose rules we unite. BELIEVE FIRMLY - ACT FAITHFULLY AND PRAY FRUITFULLY, LET US UTILIZE THE POWER OF DIVERSITY OF BELIEF THROUGH THE POWER OF PRAYERS, TO FIND THE POWER OF UNITY — TRUTH.

THE STATE OF THE STATE MESSAGE

Delivered to a joint session of the
Oklahoma Legislature, January 5, 1971

Lieutenant Governor [George] Nigh, Speaker [Rex] Privett, President Pro Tem Finis Smith, Honorable members of the 33rd Oklahoma Legislature, guests, my fellow OKIES, ladies and gentlemen:

Welcome back to Oklahoma City for the start of the Fifth Annual Session of the Oklahoma Legislature.

Eight years of public service to the people of Oklahoma will end for me next week. I value very much this honor and these years, and I thank you for the cooperation I have received--as a Senator, and most particularly the last four years as Governor of Oklahoma.

The record in this administration is your record and mine combined with the efforts of the entire executive and judicial branches of government, and thousands of concerned citizens of Oklahoma.

Most of you looked for solutions to state problems through a democratic point of view--I from a republican viewpoint. This competitive difference, I believe, brought out the best in each of us.

You looked for solutions from the point of view of your constituents in your districts, as well as for the benefit of the entire citizenry--I from the point of view of all the citizens.

Because of an embryo two-party system--not in spite of it--we have had a competitive yet harmonious relationship. 56 vetoes with only 3 final overrides attests to this fact. This relationship has produced a good record--your record, mine, and that of the executive and judicial branches of Oklahoma state government--the record of this administration.

This record is the State of the State of Oklahoma, to which I am required by the Constitution to address myself.

During the four years of this administration, there was a grand total of $1,116,148,346 dollars appropriated by the legislature. this represents a 46.4% increase over the appropriations during Governor [Henry] Bellmon's administration, and an increase of 81.6% over the four years of Governor [J. Howard] Edmondson.

During the four years of this administration, from fiscal 1967 to 1971, total appropriations increased by $141.8 million, or 65.3%.

Some of the reasons for this tremendous growth in the state's appropriate revenue are a general growth in the state's economy, an amendment to the budget balancing act, an increase in the cigarette and tobacco taxes, and a more vigorous collection of taxes by the State Tax Commission. For example, 27,700 more state income tax returns were filed last year as compared with the previous year.

Reviewing the major functions of state government reveals some astounding accomplishments over the last four years.

Appropriations to our education system increased by 81.9%, public health and assistance increased by 82.8%, mental health was up 29%, social services up 19%, public safety increased 63%, our highway program increased by 27%, the regulatory services had an appropriation increase of 70%, and natural resources rose 71%.

All of those growth and expansion in the services state government provides its citizens has been accomplished over the last four years without a general state increase. We have experienced economic growth, and we have learned to stretch the tax dollar by bringing better efficiency and economy to state government.

During the four years of this administration, a total of \$711,771,000 dollars has been, or will be, invested in new or expanded industry in 67 of the state's 77 counties. According to the companies involved, this industrial growth has created, or will create, more than 37,000 jobs. A world trade specialist, added in 1970 to the staff of the Industrial Development and Park Department, will develop foreign trade for Oklahoma companies.

For the first time in Oklahoma history, the available labor force in our state pass the one-million mark--in each of the last two years.

Employment has increased to an estimated 994,000 in 1970. This is an increase of approximately 4,600 over 1969, and is 71,600 more than in 1966, or a 7.8% increase over the four years.

This phenomenal growth and expansion of Oklahoma's economy has been the work of a most competent industrial development team in state government, coupled with hundreds of leaders at the local level. There is a new enthusiasm in rural Oklahoma--an enthusiasm that is generated by its proven ability to attract industry and job opportunities. It has shown leadership and civic pride by making the small communities of Oklahoma attractive to industry "on the grow." They now face the future with confidence and hope.

Assisting in the economic development of Oklahoma are several programs. The Ozarks Regional Commission has spent \$4.8 million dollars in Oklahoma over the past four years. Oklahoma had the first Economic Development Administration [EDA] District west of the Mississippi. We now have 6 EDA Districts which have developed \$27.1 million dollars in federal programs during this administration. Last year, Oklahoma was 4th among the 50 states in EDA expenditures. The Oklahoma Commission for Full Employment, Operation PRO (Petroleum Retail

Ownership), and the OKIE-type companies were created to boost minority employment and management in the state.

Our tourism program generated an estimated $435 million dollars in expenditures in Oklahoma last year, more than half of which came from out-of-state travelers.

Six years ago, legislation was being prepared to sell the state lodges because of their large indebtedness and low profits. Last year, not only was the debt paid off two years in advance, but $690,000 is currently being spent to refurbish the lodges.

The Management Study of State Government is saving the state an estimated $270 million dollars a year by stretching the tax dollar, producing additional revenues, and using sound business practices. New programs such as the consolidation of data processing and the creation of a state motor pool were started. The Department of Community Affairs and Planning was created in 1970 to lend state expertise to the local communities in implementing federal programs, overall planning, and coordinating with both the state and federal government. The program for emphasizing state-chartered banks has increased the number from 199 to 231, thus keeping more money in the state. The investment of idle state funds, handled by the Land Office, resulted in $355,000 additional income in two years. And the rentals charged on public school lands were made more realistic, providing an increase of $750,000 annually. These two increases directly benefit the school children of Oklahoma. The School Land Office operates a greatly expanded program with eight fewer employees. Oklahoma leads all 19 states having insurance funds with the greatest percentage of yield from invested monies. A half-million dollar refund--the largest in history--was made in 1970 to public agencies which buy workmen's compensation insurance from the state. The State Highway Department is currently responsible for a program increased by $25 million, yet administered by 126 fewer employees than in December 1966. The administration's efforts to earn an equitable rate of interest on the taxpayers' money on deposit in Oklahoma banks was instrumental in an increase in state revenues of over $5 million dollars a year.

Other governmental reforms include the complete overhaul of our penal system. The Department of Corrections was created in 1967 and is now involved in innovative programs, such as the pre-release centers and the Link Committee, to cut the recividism rate. During the last four years, our inmate population has increased by one-third, while appropriations increased by one-half. The number of probation and parole officers has increased from 13 to 58, increasing the number under supervision from under 1,000 to over 6,000. Construction is under way on a diagnostic evaluation center for adults at McAlester, and on a similar facility for juveniles at the Hissom Home in Sand Springs.

Oklahoma's judicial system also was revamped during this administration, and Oklahoma is now considered a leader among states in court reform. Judicial salaries were increased significantly; Supreme Court and Court of Criminal Appeals judges now run on their record; and other judicial races are non-partisan. One of the initial acts of my administration was the establishment of a voluntary Judicial Nominating Commission to recommend qualified persons for appointment to judicial vacancies. In 1967, our constitution was changed to adopt this concept for appointment of our appellant judges.

Oklahoma, the only state in the nation to administer its own Office of Economic Opportunity [OEO] without going through a regional office, is reaching the poor more effectively than other states. This is known by the federal government as the "Oklahoma Plan". The state OEO Youth

Program has received national recognition. Among other things, we appointed the first Youth Advisory Council.

In order to guarantee equal rights to all our citizens, the Civil Rights Act was passed during this administration. The first black-owned bank was opened in Tulsa in 1970 and is one of only 27 in the nation. The first black judge and the first blacks on the A & M Board of Regents and the Tulsa Junior College Board of Regents were appointed by this administration. The first five blacks are now on the Highway Patrol.

The Oklahoma Indian Affairs Commission was created and the first Oklahoma Indian Trade Fair was held during this administration.

One of the hallmarks of this administration has been the unprecedented support of our common school education system. Appropriations increased by 89.3% over the last four years, the biggest increase in state history. A grand total of more than $364 million dollars was appropriated to common school education during this administration.

For the first time, state monies were appropriated for school counselors, special education, and kindergartens. The number of school counselors has increased from 370 to 540 over the last four years. The number of students receiving special education has increased by 191.1%, from 14,117 to an estimated 41,200 during the four years. The number of kindergarten teachers has increased by 83%, and the number of kindergarten students has increased by 51%.

The average teacher's salary increased by $1,565 and our teachers' retirement program was so completely overhauled that it is now regarded as one of the finest in the nation. In essence, the retirement benefit for a teacher with 40-years of experience has increased during this administration from $180 a month to $340 a month, an increase of 88%.

Oklahoma ranks second in the nation in enrollment with 95.7% of our children between the ages of 5 and 17 enrolled in school. Seventy percent of our high school graduates go to college, compared with the national average of only 62%.

Appropriations to the State System of Higher Education increased by 66.1% during this administration. Faculty salaries rose by 31.9%. The first new, fully state-supported institution of higher education in Oklahoma in 50 years began operating during this administration when Tulsa Junior College opened its doors last fall. We greatly increased the output of health and medical technicians to match the needs of the state. This includes a program to increase the output of doctors by 50%. Last falls' freshman class at the University of Oklahoma School of Medicine enjoyed a 35% increase in enrollment. We also began a rural medical education scholarship fund to attract graduating doctors to the rural areas of Oklahoma. A new closed-circuit televised instructional program will soon bring post-graduate courses from four Oklahoma campuses to industrial communities of Oklahoma. Our colleges and universities confer 20% more bachelors', masters', and doctors' degrees than the average state on a population basis. The first state funding of the Student Loan Program began during this administration, guaranteeing $13.9 million in loans to 13,355 students. And plans are underway for the Oklahoma School of Dentistry to open its doors in the fall of 1971.

Our vocational-technical education program has grown from four to 15 schools in the last four years and is the envy of most every other state. Appropriations have increased by a remarkable 121%. Skilled training, tailor-made to the needs of new or existing industry, proved to be one of the best tools for attracting industry to Oklahoma. The first residential rural skill center in the

United States is located in the former Sulphur Job Corps Center.

Our State Library system saw its appropriation increased by 83%, enabling the number of counties in multi-county systems to increase from 8 to 25.

Oklahoma has made a substantial investment in its youth through improving our total education system. We have made an investment in our youth and the promise they hold for all of Oklahoma's tomorrows.

Oklahoma has also taken positive steps in the last four years to preserve and protect our environment. We have passed the Scenic Rivers Act of 1980, the Clean Air Act of 1967, the Solid Waste Management Act of 1970, the Feed Yards Act of 1969, the Open Cut Reclamation Act of 1967, and other legislation allowing tax credits for pollution control investments by private industry. The Department of Pollution Control was created in 1968 and expanded in 1970. Oklahoma is among the top four states in the nation in the number of water pollution control projects constructed by municipalities. An environmental seminar was held last year at Oklahoma State University which resulted in the creation of the Environmental Quality Council. The Arkansas-Verdigris River Planning Commission of Oklahoma was created to insure the orderly development of our new waterway to the sea with particular emphasis on land use and the environment. Two Environmental Awareness Days were held as a statewide clean-up effort and educational program. We instituted a pesticide monitoring program and there has been increased funding for the environmental programs conducted by state agencies.

To better protect the lives and property of Oklahoma citizens, our state law enforcement system has been greatly improved. The Oklahoma Bureau of Investigation added six agents and all 21 agents are now trained in narcotics and drug abuse control. Last year, the Bureau presented a training course on drug abuse to 848 local police officers and approximately 475 highway patrolmen. During the first quarter of the current fiscal year, the Bureau provided laboratory support to federal, state, and local law enforcement agencies in 1,088 cases involving marijuana and other drugs. This was an increase of 79% over the same period a year ago. To coordinate the attack on drug abuse, Oklahoma was the first state in the nation to create a Narcotics and Drug Abuse Council by Executive Order.

When another training session is completed early this year, our highway patrol strength will have increased by 50%. The highway patrol also assumed the responsibility for safety in and around 20 major lakes in Oklahoma. And the Aviation Division of the highway patrol is also assisting in forest fire protection by providing a "flying watch tower" for costly forest fires in eastern and southeastern Oklahoma. Two-man highway patrol units were instituted on a limited basis.

Life as Governor meant many formal dinners for Dewey and Ann.

A statewide Law Enforcement Plan has been adopted which, along with good leadership from every segment of the population, has made Oklahoma probably the largest state in which there has not been a single death or serious injury as the result of racial or campus unrest. The Office of Inter Agency Coordination has played a significant role in this excellent record.

In highway safety, we have instituted a vehicle inspection program, a breathalyzer test for drinking drivers, a license re-examination procedures, and other safety programs. All but six high schools in the state now provide driver education courses and are--for the first time--supported by the state. In the four years of this administration, the number of highway deaths per 100 million miles driven has dropped form 5.7 to an estimated 4.6--the lowest in state history. This compares with an estimated National Highway Death rate of 5.0.

Providing additional protection for the public was the passage of the Uniform Consumer Credit Code which has eliminated "loan sharking" and has provided credit protection for the consumer. Four million dollars already have been returned to debtors in the form of check and credits. Oklahoma, the second state in the nation to receive an exemption of credit transactions from federal control, is the nation's recognized leader in consumer credit protection.

To meet the physical and mental health needs of Oklahoma, several steps have been taken. Visiting nurse service has been increased from four to 49 counties under the Department of Public Health. The Oklahoma Commission of Alcoholism was created in 1968. There were two important achievements in providing appropriate health facilities to rural Oklahoma--one at Marietta and one at Wakita. An immunization program was begun which should immunize 90% of Oklahoma's school children in the next 8 years.

Oklahoma is the second state in the nation to close a mental hospital as a result of reducing the inpatient population. The "snake-pit" era of mental health facilities in Oklahoma is long past. The Central State Community Mental Health Center in Norman, completed in July of 1969, is the first of its kind in the nation. Plans for a similar center at McAlester are under way.

To map our future plans for better health care, a comprehensive statewide health plan was initiated in 1967.

Under the State Welfare Department, we have increased the number of licensed day care centers to 696 in the last four years. The number of children in these centers has increased from 500 to 3,000. Oklahoma ranks second in the nation in the number of rehabilitation cases served per 100,000 people, and it ranks sixth in the nation in the number of cases closed. A new children's code was enacted in 1969. It modernized our laws relating to delinquent, dependent, and neglected children. The age of boys subject to the children's code was increased from 16 to 17. The Taft Mental Hospital is being renovated and used by the older boys under the children's code.

The Welfare Department, during this administration, has spent $68 million dollars on state programs previously supported by the General Revenue Fund.

Oklahoma is also a trend setter in agriculture. We were the first state in the nation to pass the Model Wholesome Meat Act in 1968. We also have attained the status of a Modified Certified Brucellosis free state, and Oklahoma is the leading exporter of registered breeding cattle. In 1967 the sales tax on farm machinery was eliminated. Also of interest to rural Oklahoma is the fact that 208 flood control structures have been built in the last four years to bring the total to 1,477 in Oklahoma. Thirty percent of the watershed dams constructed under Public Law 566 in the nation have been built in

Oklahoma. Last summer, planning for a statewide water system was initiated. This ambitious program to provide an adequate water supply to every community will cost an estimated $4 billion dollars in federal, state, and local funds over the next 100 years.

Our state's transportation system also has made considerable progress during this administration. Long range programming of highway construction was extended to five years with roads to be built on a basis of need not political promises. Of 810 miles on our interstate system, 677 miles are now open to traffic. New interstate segments of 11.8 miles and 2.5 miles for Oklahoma City and Tulsa respectively were approved by the Federal Bureau of Roads. Oklahoma ranks 11th in the nation in the number of miles of 4-lane limited access roads. A five year program for widening, improving, and maintaining 55% of our highway system was initiated during the last four years. The act of 1970 permitting the advance purchase of highway right-of-way has already resulted in a substantial savings of tax dollars.

The State Turnpike Authority constructed the 53 mile Muskogee turnpike and the 64 mile Indian Nation "B" Turnpike. And the Cimarron Turnpike has been validated by the Oklahoma Supreme Court.

In air transportation, 14 new airports have been constructed in the last four years. Oklahoma now ranks 16th in the nation in the number of airports.

And just last week, the Arkansas River Navigation Project was opened on a limited basis.

During this administration, the minimum salary of our state employees was increased by 55%, from $200/month to $310/month. The State Merit System now covers eight additional agencies or programs and 2,000 more employees. The average monthly retirement benefit for state employees is $93.58, compared with $27.83 four years ago.

Recently, health and accident insurance, plus group life of $12,000 was added.

A $99 million dollar HERO bond issue was approved by the voters for capital improvements. Sixty-seven million dollars will go for higher education.

To enrich the cultural lives of all Oklahomans, particularly those in rural areas, the Oklahoma Arts and Humanities Council was funded by the state for the first time in history.

These accomplishments in the short period of four years are the result of a team effort.

I am proud of the record established by the many capable and dedicated citizens who have occupied directorships and key positions in this administration. I would particularly like to recognize the members of my staff for their long hours of devotion. I thank them for their tireless efforts to help me and to build a better Oklahoma. This administration has demonstrated to the voters and the taxpayers of this state what hones, concerned, and dedicated state government can accomplish without a general state tax increase. I believe the record of this administration, which is reviewed in detail in the Appendix on your desks, is a record of progress, economic growth, and improved services to the citizens of Oklahoma.

As we look to the future in Oklahoma, let me share with you one of the projects my office has been working on over the last few months that could have unparalleled impact on Oklahoma in this age of space travel. [The wrap is pulled off a model of the space shuttle]

This is one of the prototypes of the space shuttle now being considered by the National Aeronautics and Space Administration. The lower half of this model is a booster rocket that is larger than the giant 747 passenger plane. The top half, riding piggy-back, is a space orbiting vehicle which is bigger than the 727 jet aircraft. These two vehicles are now in the designing stages of development. They are pollution free during take-off and in-flight because they burn hydrogen and oxygen, thus emitting only pure water. There is a good possibility that Oklahoma could become the home of the launch site for the space shuttle, as well as play a significant role in its production and maintenance.

I recently discussed the technical ramifications of the space shuttle and its orbital mechanics with Oklahoma Astronaut Thomas J. Stafford. Based on the launch azimuth and the orbital inclinations involved, Oklahoma provides both a desirable launch and recovery location.

The establishment of a space shuttle launch and recovery operation in Oklahoma would involve a substantial investment of millions of dollars and thousands of jobs over the next decade. The economic impact on our state would be tremendous. The attention that would be focused on the Sooner state would be worldwide.

Oklahoma offers a number of advantages over other states in its attractiveness for the launch site. We have good weather at higher altitudes which reduces the cost of the launch. We have an excellent transportation system with new sea ports, major rail lines, major highways, and major international airports. We have a wealth of technical and engineering expertise. Both "teams" of companies competing for the development and production contracts from NASA have plants in Oklahoma: McDonnel-Douglass and North American Rockwell-American Airlines. They also have existing facilities that will further reduce the cost of the space shuttle program.

Clinton-Sherman Air Force Base in western Oklahoma, one possible site for the installation, ranks among the top five airport facilities in the country in terms of strength, usability, and length of runway, which is 13,500 feet.

I have written members of our Congressional Delegation in Washington seeking their support for the nation's space program and Oklahoma's potential future in the National Space Transportation System.

Although I am leaving the Governor's office, I can assure the citizens of Oklahoma I will do everything within my power in the months and years ahead to promote the location of this space age facility in Oklahoma.

If this dream of a space port in Oklahoma becomes a reality, it will be the result of work by many citizens in both public and private life. It will be the culmination of efforts on the part of business executives at our major aviation companies in Tulsa, our congressional delegation, you

State Senator Denzil Garrison worked closely with fellow Republican Dewey Bartlett.

members of the Oklahoma Legislature who have built this state's capabilities for attracting such a facility, the millions of citizens of our state who have invested their work, money, and private efforts in building a better Oklahoma for future generations. It will be the product of a concern for the future of Oklahoma as expressed by an OKIE Astronaut and OKIE Governor.

As I take your leave, I feel guilty about one thing--and that is eliminating your favorite pastime--voting for a bill popular in one area, then sending the hot potato to the second floor for veto.

Perhaps on second thought, you won't be able to resist the temptation.

Inauguration Day, January 9, 1967. This historic photograph was taken of Oklahoma's living governors. (l to r) George Nigh, J. Howard Edmondson, Johnston Murray, Dewey, Raymond Gary, William J. Holloway, and Henry Bellmon.

TRIBUTE TO E.K. GAYLORD

In the United States Senate, March 6, 1973

[E.K. Gaylord was the founder of the *The Daily Oklahoman* and was one of the state's most powerful influences in the first 73 years of the 20th century]

Mr. President, the entire State of Oklahoma today pays tribute to one of its most respected citizens, Mr. E. K. Gaylord, as he celebrates his 100th birthday. A pioneer in the truest sense, both in Oklahoma Territory and in the world of journalism. Mr. Gaylord has carved out a legacy in the minds and hearts of every Oklahoma citizen and that legacy is to look to the future, to be prepared and concerned for the days ahead.

E.K. Gaylord is a man among men--a man of religious conviction, moral persuasion, determination, energy and integrity. He is a gentle man--a man of compassion, understanding, patriotism, and love of his fellow man and Oklahoma. Mr. Gaylord is a man's man-a gentle man--a gentleman.

If some future Izaak Walton of journalism writes a book on *The Complete Editor*, he would be wise to consider E.K. Gaylord, who is celebrating his 100th birthday today by putting in a full workday and sandwiching in a speech to the Oklahoma Legislature.

There are writing editors, editing editors, city-building editors, and empire-building editors and "E.K." at 100 years young still answers all these descriptions.

Ann enjoyed living in the Governor's Mansion in Oklahoma City.

FORCED BUSING WILL NOT WORK

Testimony before the United States Senate Judiciary Committee, April 10, 1973

[Forced busing was used by the courts to enforce a national policy of desegregation of public schools in the 1960s and 1970s. There was a great national debate on the merits of busing children many miles from their local neighborhood schools for the sole purpose of achieving racially balanced schools.]

First, let me make it quite clear I am for integration. I am proud of my public and private record in race relations.

The issue of forced busing became a matter of great concern to many citizens of Oklahoma in the fall of 1969. At that time the first flood of busing opposition came to a head in Oklahoma City. As Governor of Oklahoma, I was expected to take a public position. I did not want to be wrong. As I stated, I morally believe in integration. The question was whether forced busing was a proper vehicle to achieve integration.

After much study, it became obvious to me that forced busing was an unjust, unworkable experiment, and not in the best interest of integration, education, or of people, generally. At that time, I issued a detailed statement which said in part:

"Busing, however, requires the school board and/or superintendent to discriminate against some students (of each race) attempting to eliminate the results of longtime discrimination. Discrimination to eliminate discrimination is indefensible and is a cure as sick as the disease itself."

Time has vindicated that conclusion.

Busing has created a state of social and educational chaos in Oklahoma's two largest cities, Tulsa and Oklahoma City. It is one issue on which their is little division. The vast majority of people, including Oklahomans, are opposed to forced busing and cannot understand why it has not been stopped.

I'm sure most of you are familiar with the studies which have been made in the busing experiment. David J. Armor, Associate Professor of Sociology at Harvard, in an indepth studying of busing, concluded that "busing does not lead to significant, measurable gains in student achievement or interracial harmony. The available evidence thus indicates that busing is not an effective policy instrument for raising the achievement of Black students or for increasing interracial harmony." And he continues:

Dewey and Administrative Assistant Tony Garrett, 1974.

"The available evident on busing then leads to two possible policy conclusions. One is that massive busing for purposes of improving student achievement and racial harmony is not effective and should not be adopted at this time. The other is that voluntary integration programs...should be continued and positively encouraged by substantial Federal and state grants."

I have discussed busing with the superintendents of my state's two largest school systems. Both of these men are sensitive, intelligent human beings who desire excellence in education for black and whites. Both of these men have been in the trenches on busing. They have had to formulate and implement busing plans. And both are of the opinion that busing has failed. Dr. Gordon Cawelti, Superintendent in Tulsa, wrote to me that "If the government were really trying to help in this matter, much greater efforts would be made in the area of dispersal of integrated housing so that the schools could be naturally integrated. I think unless the problem is faced up to, we will see a continued 'white flight' with the consequences that have already been recognized in a city like Atlanta, which was 70% white and 30% black ten years or more ago, and today is 78% Black." Tulsa has experienced a 37% decrease in school enrollment while the suburbs have increased by 11%. Likewise, Dr. Bill Lillard of Oklahoma City states that "Public support for schools has been weakened and polarization has increased as a result of busing."

The money spent on busing could be better spent to raise the quality of education.

Which brings me to why I am here. I have introduced Senate Joint Resolution No. 47, a constitutional amendment to prohibit the forced assignment of a child to a school on account of his color. The amendment is as follows: "No public school student shall be assigned, transferred, or otherwise compelled to attend any school on account of his race, color, creed, or national origin."

I know the Committee is considering both constitutional amendments and legislation to prohibit forced busing. I support eliminating forced busing by both legislation and constitutional amendment. The former is more expeditious and easier to achieve, the latter is more sure.

The people are frustrated that government is not responsive to their will. They point to a 1971 Gallup Poll showing 77% national opposition to forced busing--with Blacks split almost evenly.

This is one of several areas of legislative prerogative invaded and confiscated by the Supreme Court. Now is the time for Congress to exert its constitutional responsibilities to represent the people.

The amendment I have proposed will work. I suggest, gentlemen, this is why we are here—to represent the people. And the people do not want forced busing.

RESPONSE TO ROE VS. WADE

In the United States Senate, September 19, 1973

[The issue of abortion became one of the most emotional and divisive issues in American politics in the 1970's after the United States Supreme Court overturned a Texas law which prohibited the abortion of a child. *Roe vs. Wade* prevented the states from passing laws to prevent abortions under certain circumstances. The decision was talked about everywhere from the local barber shop to the halls of the United States Senate.]

Mr. President, the distinguished Senator from New York, [Mr. William F. Buckley] has, in his introduction of the human life amendment, dealt eloquently with the various aspects of the recent Supreme Court decision on abortion. As a cosponsor of the amendment, I add my voice to his and present my personal feelings on the Court's decision.

Though Chief Justice [Warren] Burger says: Plainly the Court today rejected any claim that the Constitution requires abortion on demand.

The first and most important point to be observed is that the decision does pave the way for abortion on demand for the first 6 months of pregnancy or until viability. In the first 3 months, or first trimester, according to the Court, the abortion question is totally up to the woman and her attending physician. In the second trimester, the State may regulate, but not proscribe, the abortion procedure--and so for the second trimester, the decision of the pregnant woman and her physician is compelling. In the final trimester, the State suddenly takes on a "compelling interest" in the matter, and may proscribe abortion except "where it is necessary for the preservation of the life or health of the mother." But the Court then accepts a definition of health which includes "psychological as well as physical well-being," that is, "all factors--physical, emotional, psychological, familial, and the woman's age--relevant to the well-being" of the mother.

In other words, Mr. President, as woman now has a constitutional right to pursue the abortion of her unborn child if giving birth would be socially inconvenient, or would make her emotionally upset. The right to life is no longer a right, but is now dependent on the comfort and well-being of the mother. A human being is reduced to an expendable social convenience.

How did the Court arrive at such a position? It did so by a gross distortion of history, of the Constitution, and of the nature of man. Basically, the Court based the decision on its conclusions that abortion is historically neither wholly uncommon nor unlawful; the right of privacy includes the decision of a woman to terminate her pregnancy as she and her doctor desire; and the fetus, regardless of "potential" human status, is not a legal person and thus is not entitled to human rights.

Now it is true that abortion has been practiced, legally and illegally, throughout history. But slavery has been practiced throughout history, too. Should we, therefore, repeal the laws which proscribe slavery

Mr. President, the Supreme Court decision is applauded by some as "progressive," but in reality it is regressive, a throwback to the primitive and barbarian past when human life was without innate value. The Court's interpretation of history is one-sided, and this is documented in a comprehensive brief filed by the attorneys in the *Byrn vs. New York City Health and Hospitals Corp.* case which was on appeal to the Court at the time the Court handed down its decision on abortion.

Perhaps an even greater misinterpretation, Mr. President, is found in the Court's discovery of a constitutional right to privacy which includes the right of a woman to destroy her unborn child. Not surprisingly, there was much disagreement among the members of the court as to where this right of privacy is situated-- some found it in the ninth amendment; others found it in the first, fourth, or fifth, even the entire Bill of Rights. However, the majority "felt," to use its own language, that this right is contained in the 14th amendment's concept of personal liberty and limited government.

In order to find this right in the 14th amendment, the Court has had to totally ignore the expressed intent of the Framers. Justice [William] Rehnquist in his dissenting opinion pointed out that at the time of the adoption of the 14th amendment there were 36 laws enacted by State or territorial legislatures limiting abortion, and he declared--

"The only conclusion possible from this history is that the drafters did not intend to have the Fourteenth Amendment withdraw from the States the power to legislate with respect to this matter."

Finally, after misinterpreting history and the Constitution, the Supreme Court has thrown both established scientific fact and common sense out the window by declaring that the fetus is not a legal person and thus not entitled to human rights.

The Court is unequivocal on this matter:

...The word "person", as used in the Fourteenth Amendment, does not include the unborn.

And they are aware that the validity of their case hinges on this point:

If this suggestion of personhood is established, the appellant's case, of course collapses, for the fetus' right to life is then guaranteed specifically by the Fourteenth Amendment.

Given these conditions, one would expect a thorough and cogent analysis. What is evidenced in the decision, however, is a jumble of illogic and confusion. The basic question to be resolved, before one can even begin to consider the rights of unborn children, is the issue of when human life begins.

Dewey Bartlett, the fighter pilot.

But the Court chose to totally disregard this matter by saying:

When those trained in the respective disciplines of medicine, philosophy, and theology are unable to arrive at any consensus, the judiciary, at this point in the development of man's knowledge, is not in a position to speculate as to the answer...We need not resolve the difficult question of when life begins.

Now, as a matter of fact, there is considerable agreement among scientists, biologists, philosophers, and theologians as to when human life begins. It begins at the moment of conception: when the ovum is fertilized by the sperm--forming that unique genetic organism called the zygote--fetus--which 7 days later implants itself in the womb.

It is for the "discomforts of pregnancy" that the Court is now willing to sacrifice innocent human life. The right to life is no longer an inalienable right, but a matter of chance.

Mr. President, as soon as one questions the value of human life, there is nothing in principle that prevents him from expanding the circumstance under which human beings may be exterminated. It is only a matter of degree to shift from the extermination of the fetus to the extermination of children with birth defects to the extermination of the elderly, the sick, the crippled, and others who are "less than whole persons."

Mr. President, one must always value human life. The right to life is not the gift of a state, a judiciary, or any other organization or individual. It is innate in the nature of man.

The decision of the Supreme Court is a direct attack on this fundamental human right. It is offensive not only to common sense and established scientific fact, but to that precious moral tradition which is the product or ages of human endeavor--a moral tradition which has culminated in the American philosophy. It places the rights and liberties of each individual and all human life ahead of the state.

To hold that many of us can solve our problems only by killing others is a blow to human development and justice.

Mr. President, I urge my colleagues to join me in supporting the human life amendment. Nothing less is at stake than that respect for the dignity and sanctity of human life which is the prime characteristic of a free and civilized society such as ours.

MISSING IN ACTION

In the United States Senate, December 20, 1973

[Even though the Vietnam War was over and thousands of prisoners of war had been returned to America, Senator Bartlett asked the nation in 1973 not to forget servicemen and women who were still listed as missing in action.]

Mr. President, yesterday the Senate passed my resolution calling on the people of our Nation, during this Christmas season, to give a special remembrance through our thoughts and prayers for the 1,163 members of the Armed Forces who remain unaccounted for in Indochina and for the families and friends of these men.

This past year has been especially trying for the families of our men who are still officially listed as missing in action. While the Nation celebrated and wept with joy at the return of most of our POW's last spring, the families of 1,163 men celebrated too. But privately they weep that their MIA is not on a returning plane.

The worst part of all this is that it is so unnecessary. North Vietnam can at anytime resolve the mystery of many of the 1,163 men. Yet North Vietnam has displayed utter disregard for basic humanity and justice.

Article 8B of the Paris Peace Treaty signed January 27, 1973 provides:

> The parties shall help each other to get information about those military personnel and foreign civilians of the parties missing in action, to determine the location and take care of the graves of the dead so as to facilitate exhumation and repatriation of the remains, and to take any other such measures as may be required to get information about those still considered missing in action.

Yet North Vietnam contemptuously turned her back on these provisions and have allowed the families of 1,163 men to suffer the torment of wondering whether a husband, son, brother, or friend is languishing in a prison, suffering in a hospital, or dead in a grave.

Mr. President, I would urge that the administration continue to use every diplomatic avenue possible to assist in obtaining information about these men. The families must know that we will not be satisfied until every man is accounted for.

Mr. President, the 1,163 men and their families have suffered through many lonely, sad Christmases. But they have been very brave.

At this time, I call on the U.S. Senate and all Americans to keep these men and their families in our thoughts and prayers throughout this Christmas season.

Let us also pray that another year will not pass without a full accounting of each of these men who have suffered for each of us.

AFRO-AMERICAN HISTORY WEEK

In the United States Senate, March 11, 1974

Mr. President, about a year ago, I cosponsored a bill introduced by the distinguished Senator from California (Mr. Allen Cranston) to authorize the President to designate Afro-American History Week, Senate Joint Resolution 56. More than one year has passed, and no action has been taken.

Mr. President, I want today to reaffirm my support for this measure. I expressed my desire to see action taken in a letter to Senator Roman Hruska, of the Subcommittee on Federal Charters, Holidays, and Celebrations.

Afro-American history is a discipline which has just begun to be compiled. To demonstrate my point, I wish to place in the Record a list of the accomplishments of some black Oklahomans.

Bear in mind, Mr. President, that this list is comprised of Oklahomans, only. It is a short list. Space will not allow the complete outline of all Black Oklahomans many accomplishments. Further, remember that this list must be multiplied 50 times. The need for an Afro-American history week is therefore obvious.

I urge the Senate to take action on Senate Joint Resolution 56, and thereby to formally honor the many significant Afro-American contributions to our great American heritage.

Mr. President, I ask unanimous consent that the list of accomplishments be printed in the Record.

There being no objection, the list was ordered to be printed in the Record, as follows:

Outstanding Black Oklahomans (The following brief biographical sketches are not meant to constitute a catalog of Black accomplishment; rather, they are a representative sampling of the talented and capable Black Oklahomans who have achieved national and sometimes international success,, and renown, for themselves and brought credit to all Oklahomans).

Education--Dr. Hillard A. Bowen: Dr. Bowen was born in Oklahoma City in 1911. He graduated from the Old Douglass High School and was awarded a scholarship to Langston University and later to Wilberforce, where he earned his bachelor's degree. Later, he obtained his master's degree and his Doctor of Philosophy (Ph.D.) from Ohio State University. Dr. Bowen's experience in the field of education has been wide. He was an instructor, Dean of Men, and Director of Student Personnel at Langston; a professor and registrar at Fort Valley State College in Georgia; Chairman of the School of Education at Tennessee Agricultural and Industrial State University, presently he is assistant superintendent of the Atlanta Public Schools in Georgia.

Music--Earl Grant: Mr. Grant was born in Idabel, one of 12 children of Rev. J. G. Grant. He started playing the piano and organ at the age of four during his father's church service. Accomplishments: He won national fame while playing at the Pigalle Club in Los Angeles. He performed in the United States, Japan, Australia, Europe, Mexico, and Canada. During his career, Grant appeared in such movies as "Tender is the Night," "Imitation of Life," and "Tokyo Night."

Art--John Wesley Arterbery: Born in Texas and educated in Oklahoma--Langston, University of Oklahoma. Accomplishments: Received the Letziser medal as the most outstanding art student for 1955-56 while at

Oklahoma City. he has exhibited his work very widely throughout the United States and is well known i*n art circles.* He is listed in *American Negro Art* and *Famous Negroes Past and Present.*

Jack Jordan: Like Mr. Arterbery, Jack was born in Texas and educated in Oklahoma--Ardmore's Douglass High School, Langston University and University of Oklahoma. Accomplishments: Mr. Jordan specializes in sculpture and his exhibited his work in three countries and twenty-four states. He has received more than thirty awards for his creations. He has been included in numerous books on outstanding Black artists and also in *Who's Who in American Education.*

Business--Jesse B. Blayton: Mr. Blayton was born in Harden, Oklahoma. Attended Langston University, L.L. B. University, Chicago, CPA American Ext School of Law. Accomplishments: Co-founder of Mutual Federal Savings and Loan, Atlanta, Georgia, and president since 1956. President J. B. Blayton and Company, CPA, Director of Citizens Trust National Bank and Trust Company. In 1961 he was named the most outstanding Alumnus of Langston University. Listed in *Who's Who in America.*

Sports--Marques Haynes: Mr. Haynes is a native of Sand Springs, Oklahoma. Attended Langston University and Booker T. Washington High School. After College, Mr. Haynes played for the Kansas City Stars Basketball Team, a farm team for the famous Harlem Globe Trotters. He later organized his own team, The Magicians. The Magicians have played all over the world and have gained the respect of Athletes everywhere for their skill on the he court, as well as their showmanship. He travels more than 55,000 miles a year, but he still spends a part of his off-season in Oklahoma.

Prentice Gautt: Oklahoma City--home town. Attended Page Elementary School, Douglass High School, Oklahoma University. Accomplishments: First Black to end the all-white team at O.U. Played with the Cleveland Browns, St. Louis Cardinals, All American Squad Assistant Football Coach at the University of Missouri, and Chief Scout for that team.

History--John Hope Franklin: Mr. Franklin was born in Rentiesville, a small, all Black town in eastern Oklahoma. Attended Washington High School in Tulsa, Fist University, Harvard University. Accomplishments: he taught at Harvard, Howard University in Washington, at Brooklyn College, Cambridge England, University of Chicago. In addition to teaching and writing, Dr. Franklin lectures all over the world, "from Southeast Asia to Salzburg, Austria," according to *Life Magazine.* Dr. Franklin is a prolific writer. He has ten books to his credit, including the well-known *From Slavery to Freedom.* Dr. Franklin himself is generally considered to be one of the foremost American historians.

Literature--Ralph Ellison: Mr. Ellison was born in Oklahoma City. After dropping out of high school, he attended Tuskegee Institute in Alabama. Accomplishments: Published several short stories and essays in various journals and popular magazines. His first book, Invisible man, won the National Book Award, the Russwurm Awards-1953, and the National News Publishers Award 1954. Mr.. Ellison received the Medal of Freedom from President Lyndon Johnson and the *Chevalier Ordre Arts et Lettres* from the French government for his contribution to the literature of the world.

He has taught in a number of universities in Europe and the United States. He was a charter member of the National Council on the Arts and the Carnegie Commission on Education Television. He is a Fellow in the National Institute of Arts and Science, and Silliman College, Yale University.

Other Outstanding Black Oklahomans: There are numerous other Blacks who lived in Oklahoma that have played an important role in helping to bring about better race relations in education, employment, housing, voting rights, and many other areas, to mention a few:

The Late Roscoe Dungee, Black Dispatch, Oklahoma City.

The Late Amos T. Hall, Attorney, Tulsa.

The Late Ben H. Hill, Minister, Tulsa.

The Late H. W. Williamston, Dentist, Idabel.

Ada Lois Fisher, Chickasha, Oklahoma

The Late George McLaurin, Oklahoma City

J.J. Simmons, Oil, Muskogee.

F.D. Moon, Educator, Oklahoma City.

The Late I.W. Lane, former Mayor, of Red Bird, Oklahoma

A.C. Hamlin, first Black to serve in the State Legislature.

Lucious Selmon, Eufaula, Oklahoma...placed Eufaula in the limelight--O.U. Football, All-American Guard.

The Late B.C. Franklin, Attorney, Tulsa.

Dewey and Ann at the Inaugural Ball, January 9, 1967.

THE DEATH PENALTY

In the United States Senate, March 13, 1974

Mr. President, I want to thank the Committee on the Judiciary and the administration on the excellent job they have done on preparing legislation to reimplement the death penalty for certain prescribed crimes. I am proud to be a cosponsor of this legislation.

In striking down the death penalty the Supreme Court in *Furman vs. Georgia* weaved what appeared to be an insoluble maze around capital punishment. Senate Bill 1401 appears to have avoided the multiple hazards of the Furman case and will give the judiciary the means to impartially impose the death penalty for the commission of the most serious crimes.

The 1972 Furman case exposed the inconsistencies, the unfairness, and the discrimination which unfortunately was present in many capital punishment cases prior to that time.

It is impossible to completely eliminate human frailty and error from our criminal justice system. So long as man drafts and executes our laws they will not be perfect.

But Senate Bill 1401, by carefully setting guidelines for the imposition of death has greatly reduced the chance for unfairness.

I have long been convinced of the deterrent value of the ultimate penalty for extreme criminal conduct in reducing the number of heinous crimes. After many conversations with law and judicial enforcement officers during my term as Governor this view was reinforced

Capital punishment is not only justified but necessary for several reasons.

Society must be in the position to protect itself from

the [Charles] Mansons, the [Lee Harvey] Oswalds, the [James Earl] Rays, and other vicious persons who prey on innocent victims.

Society should be able to express its moral outrage at the most abominable crimes by providing that ultimate punishment.

Certainly the death penalty eliminates the possibility that a Charles Manson will again wreak terror on a prison guard or other innocent bystander.

Basically, Senate Bill 1401 does the following: it provides that capital punishment be imposed for certain prescribed crimes, including treason, espionage, murder, aircraft hijacking, and kidnapping where death results. However, death cannot be imposed unless certain mitigating circumstances are absent and unless one or more aggravating factors is present. For instance, a mitigating factor would be the age of an offender. The sentence may not be imposed on anyone under 18. An aggravating factor could be the manner in which the crime was committed. For instance, a murder for hire.

I am convinced that this is one of the most important pieces of legislation which Congress will consider this year. Government has no higher responsibility than the protection of its citizens. Senae Bill 1401 will provide better protection. What we do will not go unnoticed by the criminal community. By passage of Senate Bill 1401 Congress will be saying that society will not tolerate certain types of conduct. And every potential murderer, hijacker, kidnapper will be on notice of the consequences of his conduct.

A FREE MARKET

In the United States Senate, November 26, 1974

[As a successful oilman, Bartlett used every opportunity to champion free enterprise in the oil industry. Bartlett chided the federal government for too closely controlling America's oil production.]

Mr. President, during the last 2 years, I have given many speeches before this distinguished body supporting a free market for energy in the United States, because, without a free market, this country would not have adequate supplies of energy in a reasonably short time or probably ever.

A free market is necessary to permit the normal forces of supply demand to respond to price. This is the most efficient way to allocate scarce resources and to solicit additional supplies. The U.S. Senate, by its past actions, believes this, except in the most important case of all--energy.

We, in Congress, have a duty, which we have ignored for many years, to insure the availability of adequate supplies of energy for the American consumer. The long run consequences of energy shortages would be fare more debilitating to our economy than the short term and shortsighted policies of maintaining an artificial low price for energy.

The time of cheap energy in this country and in the world is over. The Members of Congress should explain this fact to the American people. We should not continue to suggest that additional supplies are forthcoming when prices are reduced and controlled. This is misleading the American people, for they will be expecting something for nothing.

The quickest way to achieve energy self-sufficiency for this country is to establish a free market for energy. To continue as we have in the past with Government regulations and price controls would eventually ruin our domestic economy. If we continue to follow these short-sighted policies, the American people would be faced with even greater unemployment, continued high inflation and a lower standard of living.

In the United States today the price of over 60 percent of our domestic crude oil production is controlled. This two-tier system of crude oil pricing has caused tremendous inequities for producers and refiners of petroleum, and, it retards progress toward achieving energy self-sufficiency.

While I support a free market for all domestic crude oil production, I recognize that the Congress and the administration do not favor decontrolling all crude production at this moment . A logical next step, then, is to exempt from price controls all crude oil produced by secondary and tertiary recovery methods.

There are very sound reasons for this. The capital and operating costs of these methods are high and the known volumes of oil which can be recovered by applying enhanced recovery techniques are tremendous.

It is estimated that 434 billion barrels of crude oil in place have been discovered in the United States. Of this approximately 100 billion barrels have been produced to date. At the current controlled price of oil, an estimated 40 billion additional barrels will probably be recovered. This brings the total ultimate recovery at the current oil price to about 140 billion barrels, only a 32 percent ultimate recovery.

In the long run, any additional oil produced by enhanced recovery methods will replace even higher priced foreign imports. Exempt crude in the United

Dewey, Gerald Ford, Dave Bartlett.

States is currently running about $10.50 per barrel, while the landed price of foreign crude averages about $11.70 per barrel. Increased production of domestic crude will improve our balance of payments problems and reduce inflation. Further shortages of energy will cause greater inflation, more unemployment and a lower standard of living for the American people.

With the economic incentives provided by a free market, expanded interest in advanced recovery techniques and a greater effort in research and development there will be even greater progress toward recovering the very last drop of oil from our existing and potential oil fields.

Ann Bartlett, First Lady of Oklahoma, 1967.

MANDATORY RETIREMENT FOR FEDERAL JUDGES

In the United States Senate, January 29, 1975

[Article III of the United States Consititution provides for the lifetime appointment of federal judges. The framers of the Constitution thought it would keep politics out of the courts by mandating the lifetime appointment. However, controversy surrounding Article III judges surfaced almost before the ink was dry on the Constitution. That controversy reached a pinnacle in the nation in 1975.]

Mr. President I am today introducing for the Senate's reconsideration a proposed constitutional amendment establishing a mandatory retirement age for members of the Federal judiciary.

If adopted, this constitutional amendment would do the following: First, it would prohibit appointment to the Federal bench of any person who has attained the age of 70 years. Second, the amendment would require all judges to retire at the age of 70 except those judges who are now serving and who have not acquired their full retirement benefits. These judges in the latter category would be allowed to continue their service until their judicial retirement has vested.

Mr. President, the purpose and value of this proposed amendment are obvious. It just makes no sense to allow persons executing the authority and responsibility of a Federal judge to continue their duties at a time when they may not be fully capable either physically, or mentally.

Although Oliver Wendell Holmes served admirably on the Supreme Court until he was 90 and Louis Branders retired at 82, these are rare exceptions. Far too often judges being devoted to their job, far outstay the time when they can judiciously perform their duties.

Business and government have already recognized the good judgment of a reasonable retirement age. In 1966 the Congress passed legislation requiring civil service employees to retire at age 70. In most instances American businesses require retirement by age 65.

The need for mandatory retirement of judges exceeds that of most other professions. Presently judges are in the unique position of serving for life with virtually no oversight short of impeachment for commission of a crime.

There exist numerous cases of judges who, though well qualified when younger, continue to serve and handle important cases even though advancing age has brought on senility and actual incompetence.

Some would argue that, if such an amendment is passed covering the judiciary, as a corollary it should also include Members of Congress. However, there is a considerable difference between Members of Congress who must periodically face the voters and a Federal judge who is isolated from any oversight. The voters frequently retire a politician who does not have the good sense to see that he can no longer do the job. Voters do not have this opportunity with Federal judges.

Mr. President, if passed, this amendment will do a great deal to restore the public's lagging confidence in their judicial officers, for often, one senile judge has given the judiciary as a whole a black mark. I urge serious consideration of this amendment.

REPORT ON VIETNAM

A letter to the Committee on Armed Services,
March 25, 1975

Enclosed is a copy of a report on my recent trip to South Vietnam and Cambodia. I hope you may find the time to read the entire report; but, in summary, I have strongly urged that Congress vote the requested supplementary military assistance to South Vietnam and military, medical and food aid to Cambodia.

It is disturbing that the congressional leadership is adjourning for 10 days vacation without taking any action on these needed appropriation bills for Cambodia and South Vietnam. Daily the military situation in both of these countries deteriorates while scores of additional casualties are suffered because of the non-communists' lack of sufficient ammunition to defend themselves adequately.

The North Vietnamese have the largest force ever in South Vietnam--with double the number of tanks and triple the number of artillery. This huge army, in blatant violation of the Paris accords, is made possible by increased support from China and Russia. In contrast, our military aid to South Vietnam is less than half of one to one replacement of equipment and expendables. Without immediate additional military aid to Cambodia, the non-communists will be unable to hold the perimeter around Phnom Penh and will have no hope of a controlled political solution.

Without additional military aid to Cambodia, a bloodbath of unparalleled propositions is possible. This could occur while the Congress is on vacation. Although the situation is less grim in South Vietnam, it is far worse now than two weeks ago.

It is imperative that we act on aid for Southeast Asia as quickly as possible. We're now talking about a total supplementary appropriation of approximately $500 million, which is about 1/60 of what we spent in one peak year of involvement in Vietnam in the late 1960s.

If either Cambodia or South Vietnam falls because of inadequate ammunition, gasoline, medical or food supplies, our allies around the world will receive a message loud and clear. I am afraid that message will read that the United States has defaulted on its commitment to its friends.

We are facing a test of the will of this nation to provide our friends the military aid they need to defend their lives and freedom against aggression from communists supported with aid from Russia and China.

The dominoes that might tumble around the free world could be the confidence of friendly nations in the leadership ability of the United States. Additionally, this could be a national security threat to the nations of the free world.

I urge the Senate leadership to schedule votes on these bills before adjourning on Wednesday—at least on Cambodia—and, if necessary, postpone the recess a day or two. Immediate U.S. military support will strengthen the resolve of Cambodians and South Vietnamese who believe there is a big difference between free institutions and communist tyranny.

PROSECUTE DESERTERS

In the United States Senate, April 23, 1975

I was interested to find out today that many of the soldiers who deserted the American military while serving in South Vietnam are literally "coming out of the woodwork" trying to leave Vietnam and return to the United States.

Although these are men who turned their backs on the United States, I do not suggest that we reciprocate by turning ours. However, it is interesting that these men who refused to fight to stop Communist aggression are now doing everything they can to avoid the possibility of living--or dying--under a Communist regime.

No doubt, these men will take their chances through our court system versus their prospects under communism.

Even though these men are deserters, they are Americans; and basic humanitarian instincts dictate that we not abandon them as they did us.

However, upon their return to the good old U.S.A., I hope no one has the gall to suggest any blanket amnesty or alternate service outside our court system for these men who refused to serve. They have apparently violated the law. They refused President [Gerald] Ford's request that they return to United States, and now they should be prosecuted through the courts as any other person who is suspected of violating our law.

Dewey and Ann Bartlett with Pat and Richard Nixon.

NATURAL GAS FOR IRRIGATIONAL FARMING

In the United States Senate, June 17, 1975

Mr. President, I want to commend my colleagues for the interest they have shown in this important matter. In particular I would like to thank Senator [Pete] Domenici for arranging the time so we might enter into this colloquy.

The recent Federal Power Commission [FPC] ruling contained in Opinion 697A is of particular significance to Oklahoma. This is true because energy and agriculture comprise two of the great endeavors of the people of Oklahoma. Given strong dependence of modern U.S. agriculture on energy and the strong global dependence on the modern agricultural system of the United States, it is apparent that any decision which reduces the availability of energy supplies for agriculture will consequently lower the supply of food for this Nation and the world.

It is inevitable that food will become much more costly and must less abundant unless our domestic energy supplies are expanded significantly and are used efficiently. Energy must be conserved where possible. Our national energy policy must be formulated so that scarce fuels will ultimately be allocated according to the priorities of an unregulated energy market. This free market mechanism is the only way to insure both proper allocation of our energy resources and a successful effort to provide those fuels to all who desire them.

While I believe a free market for all energy in the United States is the only true and fair solution to the energy problem. I recognize that there has not been such a market in operation in the case of natural gas for over 20 years. This has caused tremendous shortages of natural gas and an apparent need for the Federal Power

Commission to institute its own allocation program. As long as this allocation system exists, it is essential that the scarce gas be distributed in a manner which is consistent both with internal restraints of the FPC's own allocation program and with our national energy goals and food production commitments.

The nature of the farm market today is such that the duplicate capital costs required for conversion to alternate fuels cannot be passed through to consumers of farm products. This is not the same kind of market that the larger industrial firms enjoy, and there is no reason to believe that a change in the nature of the farm market is coming in the future.

A several weeks delay in irrigation could cause loss of

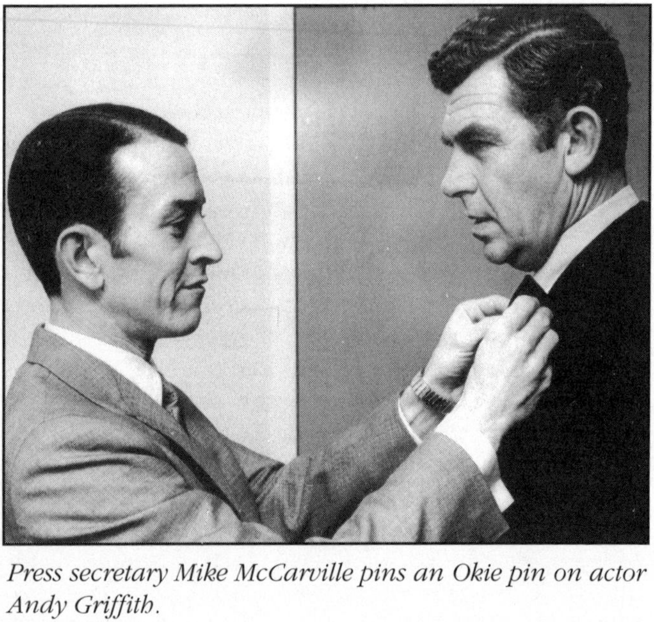

Press secretary Mike McCarville pins an Okie pin on actor Andy Griffith.

an entire crop. Farming is not an ongoing manufacturing process in which a stream of similar goods move through a plant. A crop is a once or twice a year endeavor and the farmers income depends entirely on these harvests.

Furthermore, if there is uncertainty in the supply of gas to be used for irrigation purposes, the decision as to what farming method would be pursued must be made early in the year before the gas is required. The capital requirements and fertilizing techniques for wet versus dry farming are significantly different, and it would not be possible to change from one method to another midway through the crop year.

The curtailment of natural gas for irrigation purposes would have a devastating and deleterious effect upon national, State, and local economies. This would be particularly detrimental at a time when the entire Nation is facing a significant recession. We should be particularly concerned about farm incomes because agriculture is our Nation's largest industry. It employs 4.5 million workers and produces goods worth about $243.6 billion annually.

Each year farmers spend over $57 billion to produce crops and livestock. This infusion of capital generates considerable economic activity, especially in the small towns and rural communities. On the national level, exports of agriculture commodities totaled an unprecedented $22 billion in 1974 and boosted the favorable U.S. agricultural trade balance to a record $11.8 billion. This agricultural trade balance helped to offset this country's deficit in nonagricultural products, which totaled $14.8 billion in 1974 due to the quadrupling of the price of petroleum imports.

Irrigation farming has played a major role in the overall economic contribution of our Nation's agricultural industry. The Economic Research Service has placed the number of irrigated acres harvested in 1974 at 36,280,000. This is 11.7 percent of the total harvested cropland in the United Sates, and it represents nearly 27 percent of the total harvest cropland value.

Gambling with food production and the agricultural economy of this Nation because of an ill-conceived ruling on natural gas usage, warrants the determination--and yes, the courage--of the FPC to rescind that ruling.

Dewey, Legislative Assistant David Russell, Secretary of Agriculture Earl Butz, and Senator Pete Domenici from New Mexico at the United Nations World Food Conference in Rome, 1974.

OUR FUTURE AS A WORLD POWER

In the United States Senate, May 15, 1975

[The conclusion of the Vietnam War caused American political leaders to question the role of Congress in calling the shots in foreign policy, especially during a war.]

Mr. President, when will the Congress admit its own limitations in the handling of foreign affairs? The answer to this question may be crucial to our future as a world power.

The disastrous chain of world events in recent weeks, highlighted by the fall of South Vietnam and Cambodia, have intensified doubts about America's foreign policy. While in the past, criticisms of our Nation's policies have been frequent and vocal, they were generally of a different type than the legitimate questions heard today. In the past, questions centered around the wisdom of our policies--today we are asked whether we have a policy at all. Formerly, others wondered why a specific policy was adopted--now the issue is "who makes foreign policy, the President, the Congress, or both, or neither one?" In earlier times, our manner of meeting a commitment too frequently was often challenged--In recent times, we have been challenged as to whether we have any such commitment.

The temptation in times like these is to designate a single factor, such as congressional ineptness for the outcome in Vietnam and Cambodia. For many years in the future, political scientists will be dissecting and diagnosing U.S. involvement in Southeast Asia and the ultimate debacle which occurred there. Years of analysis may be required to give the proper weight to all factors, but it is not too simplistic to say that congressional action ultimately contributed nothing in this area to preserve freedom or enhance our national power, influence, or prestige.

Regardless of analytical variations, one conclusion on which there is unamity is that we lost. Actually, what we lost is a matter of disagreement. Did we lose a war or just not win a war? Can anyone say that we did not lose national prestige? Though some may argue that prestige was lost by our entry into the Vietnam conflict, it can scarcely be argued that our prestige is now lower today as a result of the ultimate downfall of those we defended. Whether our national honor has been damaged might be subject to debate, but can anyone maintain that we have not lost credibility? Congressional vacillation, however well intended, has contributed to lossess of prestige and credibility.

Governor Bartlett and President Richard Nixon in the Oval Office of the White House.

Has there been a real, or only an apparent, loss in our commitment to freedom? Who in Congress can make a case that our commitment is stronger than the commitment of Russia and China? While we debated, the Russians and Chinese were pouring in support to their allies--and the world knows it.

Regardless of our views as to what went wrong, few Americans enjoyed the sight of our Ambassador scurrying aboard a helicopter as Saigon prepared for surrender. We are not used to an ally's defeat for any reason, much less at least accelerated because of our failure to supply needed support. Congress literally fiddled while Vietnam burned. Let us hope that we have not become accustomed to our recent role. So that there may be no misunderstanding, my position is not that we should return to the role of world policeman nor is it my view that all world problems can be neatly categorized in packages of black or white. The point is that for at least a decade, American foreign policy in Southeast Asia has left much to be desired--and that growing congressional involvement has been part of the problem rather than part of the solution.

In the days and years ahead, we, as a nation and as a government, must attempt to salvage something of value from that war. Certainly, various ingredients went into the downfall of Cambodia and South Vietnam. Many of these were out of control and must be left for the consciences of other countries, their peoples, and leaders.

No amount of finger pointing or breast-beating will rescue Vietnam or Cambodia from Communist domination. However, the role which Congress played there must be evaluated. For the future, there is one central issue to which these remarks are addressed: What is the proper role for Congress in foreign affairs?

Congress has a valid role in foreign affairs. But the danger is that the collective ego of Congress will make it impossible for Congress to realize its own serious limitations. Certainly, control of the purse strings is a proper congressional role. Congress should be able to assist in the articulation of broad policy, but realistically it must either accept the policies of the President or adopt its own--it cannot play a major role in foreign affairs by endless dialogue and hand-wringing.

The failure of Congress to declare a clear policy in Southeast Asia and to respond quickly to Presidential requests for emergency military aid raises the question of whether two committees of 535 Members can engage responsibly on a wide front of foreign affairs.

I do not know the precise role which Congress should play in foreign affairs. But we must begin a period of self-examination. Secretary [Henry] Kissinger has called for a major reassessment of American foreign policy objectives and methods. This is essential.

Obviously, one of the questions which must be explored is whether Congress made up of two committees, one with 100 members and another with 435, can effectively dance in foreign affairs. By its very nature, foreign policy must have a definite firmness, yet a reasonable flexibility capable of quick formulation and clear articulation. Is Congress inherently limited in this role? I favor extending as much as possible the effective participation of Congress in foreign affairs.

Somehow, we must restore--through a partnership between the Executive and the Congress--an unfailing confidence by which foreign governments, friend and foe alike, as well as our own citizens, will know that when the president speaks that he speaks authoritatively for the entire country.

HOSPITALS FOR RURAL AMERICA

In the United States Senate, July 15, 1975

Mr. President, today I am introducing proposed legislation to direct the Secretary of the Department of Health, Education, and Welfare [HEW] to provide up to $100,000 on a 70 to 30 matching basis to hospitals in medically underserved rural areas to assist them to upgrade their facilities so they may qualify for physician residency programs.

One of our serious problems in health care delivery is the drastic shortage of doctors in rural areas. In the United States there is an average of one physician to 750 people. This favorable ratio is made possible only because of the top heavy number of doctors in urban areas at the expense of the smaller and rural communities.

For instance, in Oklahoma we have 1 doctor for every 1,000 persons. But in Tulsa and Oklahoma City, there is 1 doctor for every 500 persons. Unfortunately, the rural areas range from 1 to 1,200 to 1 to 6,000. This is inadequate, and it leaves rural Oklahoma with, at best, inadequate health services.

Oklahoma has taken the initiative in trying to solve its rural health care problem. While I was Governor, we established a rural medical scholarship fund to attract more doctors to the rural areas. This program has been successful but is just one step in a long process.

One of the real deterrents to attracting and keeping doctors in rural areas is the lack of residency programs outside large cities. For instance, in Oklahoma there is only one residency program outside Oklahoma City and Tulsa. The significance of the lack of rural residency programs is that statistics indicate that a doctor is likely to stay in the area in which he does his residency. As a matter of fact, statistics on a nationwide basis show that

75 percent of the doctors permanently locate where they performed their residency.

This year Oklahoma will graduate 170 doctors, yet only 86 residencies are available and these are in Oklahoma City and Tulsa. Obviously, almost half of our doctors are forced to leave Oklahoma; and the chances are they will never return to work. The Oklahoma legislature enacted legislation this past session to help with this problem. Under the bill the State will pay up to $6,000 of a resident's cost to a hospital. But additional assistance is needed, to enable many hospitals to qualify for residency programs and it must come from the Federal level.

A key problem in the lack of rural residency programs is the failure of a hospital to have all of the necessary facilities. For instance, a hospital may be in every way qualified with staff yet not have a cardiac unit; and thus they will be turned down on the program.

The bill I have proposed would authorize the Secretary of HEW to provide grants of up to $100,000 to a facility on a 70 to 30 matching basis to assist them in upgrading to meet residency requirements. I think it is important that a local entity be required to furnish 30 percent of the funds to prove their commitment to a project.

Mr. President, I am convinced that this legislation will be a significant step in assisting America's rural areas to upgrade their health service delivery systems. Americans living in rural areas have the same health needs as their urban counterparts, and we should assist them in achieving that parity.

CAUTION ON ARMS CONTROL

A letter to President Gerald Ford, February 5, 1976

Dear Mr. President:

In this year's State of the Union address, you expressed hope that "a further agreement to limit the strategic arms race may be achieved." We share that hope. You also cautioned, "Only a balanced agreement will serve our interest and minimize the threat of nuclear war." We share that caution.

We are alarmed that several public figures, including a few of our colleagues, have pressed for an immediate arms accommodation with the Soviet Union. These dangerous and unnecessary demands for haste reflect an unwarranted faith that any settlement is a good settlement.

For the United Sates, a bad treaty is worse than no treaty. Proper vigilance and informal arrangements now permit the superpowers to adjust their strategic forces to political and technological change. However, a shortsighted or ambiguous agreement which prevents necessary force adjustments could lock our country into a previously avoidable nuclear confortation.

Hurried diplomacy creates vulnerability and distrust, not arms control and understanding. When questioned, we Americans rush to reveal our deepest secrets. However, we are embarrassed to question the activities of those who hide everything. For this reason, the security of our nation requires that any arms accord be easily and absolutely verifiable. Weapons systems such as strategic cruise missiles, whose range and purpose are difficult to determine without continuous inspection of every vehicle, must not be subject to limitations which can be enforced only in open societies.

The terms of any treaty must be clearly understood

by all parties so that violations can be quickly identified and corrected. Strategic bombers, launchers, heavy ICBMs [Intercontinental Ballistic Missles], MIRVed [Multiple Independently Targeted Re-entry Vehicles] missiles, and similar items must be sharply defined, and there can be no secret agreements.

Since our American nation is slow to take up arms when new threats are discovered, a sufficient margin of security must be provided to permit remedial action before irreparable harm can be done. Equality in throw weight and numbers will provide a good measure of this standard.

Each step in the advance of detente must be a test to determine whether another step should be taken. the Soviet Union must match the restraint already shown by the United States both in written agreements and in unilateral actions. Until the Soviet Union ends its massive deployment of increasingly accurate heavy ICBMs, the option to improve and increase our own, much smaller ICBM force must not be restricted.

Disorder on all continents reminds us that two hundred years of successful democracy have not yet guaranteed the survival of the American republic. In this significant year, any strategic arms limitations will receive rigorous public examination and evaluation. Given the difficult issues which remain to be settled, we ask you to instruct the Secretary of State that negotiations should continue without regard to ill-advised demands for an immediate agreement.

Respectfully yours,
DEWEY F. BARTLETT

VIOLENCE IN LABOR DISPUTES

In the United States Senate, March 25, 1976

[Bartlett was vehemently opposed to violence by union members during labor disputes. He introduced a bill to give federal courts jurisdiction over violence during a labor dispute.]

Mr. President, according to some predictions, the year ahead may be one of special difficulty in the negotiation of contracts with organized labor. While there may be nothing Congress can do to facilitate these negotiations, there is something we can do to help insure against the violence which often results from labor disputes.

Certainly, destruction of property, threats to the well-being of individuals and even personal injury or death are covered by State and local laws; but as history has shown, local law enforcement personnel and courts are unable to handle the necessary enforcement to protect those involved, both from their own actions and from outside influences.

The Hobbs Act was adopted in 1949 in an attempt to curb the use of violence in labor disputes. This act was the result of an already existing history of violence. However, even this did not prove effective, and the Supreme Court in 1973 provided the direction to Congress as to the proper corrective legislative action, the missing link in the act to bring this continuing violence under control. The invitation is stated explicitly in a concurring opinion by Justice [Harry] Blackman: I readily concede that my visceral reaction to immaturely conceived acts of violence of the kind charged in this indictment is that such acts deserve to be dignified as federal crimes. That reaction on my part, however, is legislative in nature rather than judicial. If Congress wishes acts of that kind to be encompassed by a federal statute, it has the constitutional power in the interstate context to effect that result.

There are ample illustrations of violence, and I am not talking about the cases of simple vandalism such as a brick thrown through a window. On January 15, 1976, labor-related violence was making the news. A Lake Charles, La., plant was the site of a dispute by two unions over representation at a construction site. This dispute did not involve the company or wages and benefits. It was a "simple" conflict over which union would represent the workers. The result of this "simple" conflict was the death of one man and physical injury to five others. Also, damage was caused to tow trailers, a pickup truck, a dozen automobiles, and a guard house. At the present time, a grand jury has been convened in Lake Charles to investigate the death and related property destruction. The district attorney's office reports that 29 indictments have been returned, and the investigation is continuing.

This identical representation dispute was also being carried on at another of the contractor's projects. This was a refinery site in Houston, Tex., and the violence over three days resulted in approximately $1 million in damages. The dispute in Houston has not subsided. Since January, one person has been nearly beaten to death; and while this was occurring, the plant nurse was locked in her aid hut from the outside so that she was unable to assist injured individuals. The only charges filed so far in Houston resulted from attacks on persons with the media who were covering the violence. The whole situation is currently under investigation by the Special Crimes Bureau of the Houston district attorney's office.

Who pays for an individual's car that is riddled with bullets while parked in front of the home during off-work hours? How do we compensate a person for his or her mental anguish and that of the family when their home is attacked with bombs or bullets shot through the window?

A number of construction projects have been the scene of substantial destruction. The issue may have been union representation, wages, hours, or fringe benefits, but the result was the same--the individuals and the public must eventually pay for the cost. These scenes are like pieces out of what are now classified as overly violent movies and television shows. Movies and television shows with this sort of violence would be severely criticized by a large part of our society and given ratings such as R or not shown during prime time.

These situations cannot be condoned or simply overlooked. Justice mandates Congress to follow the direction given by the Supreme Court in *United States vs. Emmens* to amend the Hobbs Act; namely to amend the provisions of the act to specifically provide for Federal jurisdiction in situations where excessive violence has occurred.

It is literally impossible to obtain a tally of the cost of such violence to the American economy; and in many cases, it is impossible for local law enforcement officials to take action to prevent such destruction or to prosecute those responsible after the fact.

There are a number of reasons that can be cited for the lack of action by local law enforcement, but what it comes down to is that they need assistance because they simply cannot handle the problems that exist. This is one example where the Federal Government can strengthen and complement.

Senate Bill 2795, which I introduced on December 16, 1974/5, is not directed at the isolated incident of minor vandalism but rather to acts of violence that result in substantial damage. The damage must exceed $2,000 before this new provision would come into effect. This would prevent a vast expansion of Federal jurisdiction and retain a large amount of local authority and autonomy.

The second safeguard in my bill is that in order for the destructive action to be a Federal crime it must have been a willful act.

Third, my bill will safeguard the original jurisdiction of States in criminal matters. The bill does not seek to usurp the jurisdiction of a State when criminal actions have been taken by parties involved in the labor dispute; however, my bill does provide the assistance of the Federal Government in cases of substantial physical damage which, in many cases, would involve other criminal acts. In other words, the services of the Federal Government would be available in cooperation with local law enforcement authorities to fully investigate all incidents of major violence.

The Congress is responsible to the wishes of the people they represent. My amendment will answer the directive of the Court and meet our responsibility to the demands of the public.

THE B-1 BOMBER

In the United States Senate, May 10, 1976

Mr. President, I rise in support of the B-1 bomber—a program which should rank high on our list of national priorities. The continued development and procurement of the B-1 will help insure that this country is capable of fulfilling its most important obligation to its people; namely, that of guaranteeing the survival of this Nation as a free and independent society.

Since the inception of the B-1 program, the Department of Defense [DOD] has shown that its development approach has been both sound and practical. The DOD has conducted and provided to the Congress detailed and extensive analyses of the B-1 and alternative aircraft candidates.

Joanie and Ann Bartlett, 1960.

The critics of the B-1 have been numerous, vociferous, and wrong. Some have argued against the cost-effectiveness of the B-1 compared to other alternatives. For example, a recent study by the Brookings Institute, although acknowledging the importance of maintaining bombers in our strategic forces, claims that the future threat to penetrating bombers will be more readily accommodated by heavy reliance on cruise missiles than with the current DOD program which includes the B-1. Yet, even today the Soviets are known to have mobile low altitude-capable SAM's [surface to air missles] against which, the authors acknowledge, the cruise missiles are ineffective without prior suppression; the authors further admit that suppression cannot be assured if the SAM's are mobile. In addition, the study exaggerates the cost of deploying the B-1 by burdening it with the cost of a new tanker fleet on the basis that KC-135's are being given to our Reserve Forces. In fact, the Reserve Forces are not only being given the KC-135's, but also the same mission of refueling our strategic aircraft as was accomplished previously by our Active Forces. The Air Force has also testified that it see no need for a new tanker for the B-1. Lastly, the performance characteristics attributed to cruise missiles by the study are not support in referenced DOD testimony and are optimistic compared to engineering estimates from the DOD development programs.

Some critics claim that the B-1 costs too much and that the costs are on the rise. Yet the facts as presented to the Congress reaffirm that the B-1 cost has remained relatively constant in non-inflated dollars. The original program cost estimate in June 1970 was $9.9 billion versus the current estimate--in the same dollars--of $11.4 billion--a cost growth of only 12 percent over a period of almost 6 years. A better measure of cost control by the

DOD is the fact that the current B-1 cost estimate is the same as that made in December 1973. Most important, however, is the fact that the B-1 program cost has not risen since the completion of the DOD cost-effectiveness analysis; thus it is clear the B-1 continues to remain the most cost-effective alternative to maintaining our strategic bomber force capabilities.

Other critics claim the B-1 will not perform as advertised. Let me address that issue. The B-1 engineering development program has evolved flexibly in an attempt to minimize research and development expenditures prior to any commitment to production and to facilitate an orderly transition from development to production once a production reviews of the B-1 program have shown that, although some program adjustments were necessary, the B-1 program was sound, and there were no major technical problems which would preclude successful development. Moreover, the program continues under close scrutiny by both the Office of the Secretary of Defense and the Congress.

In summary, Mr. President, I believe that it is important, indeed incumbent, for the Congress to support the B-1 bomber program. This action would signal clearly to the U.S.S.R. the United States' resolve about remaining No. 1 in military preparedness, and would endorse the Triad concept for our strategic nuclear forces.

Dewey loved relaxing in his backyard, 1960

PANAMA CANAL TREATY

In the United States Senate, September 10, 1976

[Senator Bartlett was in favor of sitting down at the negotiating table with the government of Panama to revisit the issue of American control of the Panama Canal. Little did he know that his suggestion would trigger a hot national debate.]

Mr. President, in 1903 the people of the United States accepted one of the great challenges of our history when we entered into an agreement with the Republic of Panama to construct a shipping passageway connecting the Atlantic and the Pacific Oceans. This had been a dream of all people of our hemisphere for decades, and it was to the United States that the world turned for help in realizing this dream.

This construction of the canal would take U.S. Army engineers 10 years to complete, at a cost of 4,000 lives and $310 million. Because of this tremendous cost in terms of human and financial resources, America did not accept this challenge lightly. We committed ourselves to the task not solely as a benefactor to the lesser nations who would share in the rewards of our adventure, but primarily because we knew that such a passageway could be immensely valuable to America's economic and national defense interests.

We also knew that some firm and everlasting assurances would be required to provide for those interests after the completion of the canal. We did not undertake this project with the understanding that we might have access to the canal for a few years or a few decades, subject to the discretion of other nations. America accepted the challenge only under a set of conditions which would be for a project that was inalienable and forever worthwhile.

We undertook construction of a canal across the Isthmus of Panama only after these conditions were set forth and agreed upon by the United States and the Republic of Panama in the signing of the Hay-Bunau-Virilla Treaty in December 1903.

This treaty granted to the United States "in perpetuity the use, occupation, and control" of a specified zone of land through Panamanian territory for the construction, operation, and defense of a ship canal; the treaty afforded the United States "all the rights, power, and authority within the zone ...which the United States would possess and exercise if it were the sovereign of the territory ...to

Dewey and Ann meet with their supporters at a victory party on election night, November, 1966.

the entire exclusion of the exercise by the Republic of Panama of any such sovereign rights, power or authority;" provided for payment of U.S. compensation to Panama in the amount of an initial $10 million and an annual annuity of $250,000.

For some time now the Republic of Panama has expressed an interest in renegotiating the Canal Treaty with the United States. Our country has acted in good faith in attempting to comply with the wishes of Panama while still protecting the interests of the United States.

Beginning in 1964, under President [Lyndon] Johnson, the attitude of each succeeding administration has been that the United States should negotiate a new treaty with Panama which would abrogate the 1903 treaty. Negotiations continued from 1965 until 1967 at which time it was announced that three draft treaties had been agreed upon by the two countries. However, no action was ever taken on these treaties by either country apparently because of premature publication of the terms of the treaties in the press, as well as the fact that both countries were in the midst of major election campaigns at that time. In 1968, Gen. Omar Torrijos took power in Panama through a coup and in 1970 flatly rejected the draft treaties previously agreed to, but did indicate a willingness to pursue further negotiations on the subject.

Talks resumed in 1971 and have continued to the present. Progress in these negotiations has been slow because the principal objections of the Panamanians concern provisions of the treaty which were recognized in 1903 and are still recognized today as being vital to the protection of American economic and strategic interests.

Perhaps the time has come for changes in our operations of and treaty governing the Panama Canal, and I favor discussions and negotiations of some of the points of Panama's objections, specifically:

First. Panamanian use of some of the Canal Zone;

Second. The hiring of more Panamanians to work on the canal;

Third. The percentage of Panama's profits from canal revenues; and

Fourth. The United States annual annuity to Panama.

However, there are provisions of the treaty which cannot be subject to negotiation, if the U.S. commercial and strategic interests are to be safeguarded. The world has not changed so much as to alter the fundamental principles of the original Panama Canal Treaty, which legally vested sovereignty and control of the canal and Canal Zone in the United States permanently. America has faithfully honored that treaty.

We constructed, maintained, operated, and defended the canal to the benefit of all nations and at a U.S. taxpayer's net investment of almost $6 billion over the past 60 years. The continued efficient U.S. operation of the canal has resulted in major economic benefits for Panama including a major contribution to that country's economy thereby affording it the highest per capita income in Central America.

Furthermore, Panama's history of political instability, her inadequate military defense capability, and lack of technical and managerial skills demonstrate that Panama does not possess the capacity to manage, operate, and defend effectively the canal.

As we continue to discuss and negotiate changes in the operation of the canal with the Republic of Panama, I believe the United States must insist on retaining the provisions in the treaty which guarantee our rights "in perpetuity" rather than agreeing to surrender these rights at a specified date in the future. We must retain our jurisdiction over the Canal Zone in order to provide for the defense of the canal. We must retain the authority to maintain within the Canal Zone the level of military personnel and equipment necessary to defend the canal. As stated more generally in the political platform of the Republican Party, the United States must not surrender any jurisdiction, territory, or property which is necessary for the protection of the United States and the Western Hemisphere.

Mr. President, I do not recognize as a valid reason for negotiating a new Panama Canal Treaty the argument that the 1903 treaty is an anachronism, a vestige of American colonialism, and that it provides a rallying point for Panamanian and other Latin American countries against the United States, or that the treaty provides a visible target for elements hostile to the United States outside the region.

Such an argument smacks of the kind of international blackmail which has become treacherously common in the world today. America will not demand the respect of other nations by yielding to such coercion. Capitulation does not work it merely whets the insidious appetites of other nations.

Let us continue our negotiation with the Republic of Panama in the spirit with which we have negotiated from the beginning, a spirit of good faith and determination to provide for the best interests of both nations without compromising the vital interests of either nation or the rest of the world.

David Albert Bartlett, pioneer oil and gas banker.

DEPARTMENT OF EDUCATION

In the United States Senate, January 19, 1977

[Bartlett introduced a bill in 1977 to establish a separate agency of the federal government to be known as the U.S. Department of Education. The giant Department of Health, Education, and Welfare administered education programs at the time of the introduction of the bill.]

The Federal Government is a major source of financial and technical assistance to the Nation's schools and colleges. Today I introduce legislation which provides for a significant administrative change in the delivery of this assistance. Currently Federal assistance is provided chiefly through the Office of Education, a major component of the Education Division of the Department of Health, Education, and Welfare [DHEW]. The Office of Education has a staff of approximately 3,000 employees and a budget of more than $7 billion. It administers more than 100 programs, most of them operated through State and local education agencies. These programs affect students in virtually all of the Nation's 16,000 school districts, 3,000 universities and two and four-year colleges, and 10,000 occupational schools.

The major goals of the Office of Education are:

To equalize the opportunity for education for all individuals and groups who are at a disadvantage because of economic, racial, or geographic conditions or physical or mental handicaps.

To improve the quality and relevance of American education, primarily through research, development, experimentation, demonstration, dissemination, and training.

To provide financial and technical support to libraries, State and local education agencies, developing institutions of higher education, and adult and vocational education.

Five Bureaus, several Staff Offices and Staffs attached directly to the Office of the Commissioner, and 10 Regional Offices work toward meeting these goals. I am sure that when one reviews the history of the Office of

Dewey Follett Bartlett, Oklahoma's 19th Governor.

Education he cannot help but be impressed with the growth and scope of operation of the agency since its inception and the tremendous progress it has made to date in fulfilling its mission.

However, I believe that a vast improvement can yet be made if the agency charged with the responsibility for carrying out this mission were given Cabinet-level status and charged with the responsibility for administering all programs under the jurisdiction of the Department of Health, Education, and Welfare directly related to education, as well as certain other education programs now administered by other Departments and Agencies. Certainly credentials of this most important agency more than qualifies it to undertake this awesome responsibility, and the importance of its mission is more than worthy of Cabinet-level status.

I am, therefore, introducing legislation to accomplish this objective. I am aware that the DHEW has historically opposed this type of legislation, citing as its reasons the opinion that a vast majority of the concerns of the Agency such as poverty, drug abuse, alcoholism, child development, rehabilitation or handicapped, are not exclusively an education problem, or a welfare problem, but involved aspects of each of these areas. It is their belief that the creation of a separate Department to administer education programs would isolate them from related programs which deal with human problems, programs with which they must necessarily remain closely lined. Further, they think such a change would result in a fragmented approach to problems bearing on the conditions of the family and the individual and the results therefrom would also be fragmented.

I disagree with this opinion and believe strongly that on the contrary a separate agency specifically charged with the responsibility for carrying out Federal policy with regard to education can only result in further improvement of the education system of this Nation. Unlike the present situation where the Department charged with carrying out health and welfare programs as well, the Department I propose would be able to devote its full attention and resources to achieving a Federal education program of the highest quality, and would still be able to work with the Health and Welfare Department in achieving this goal. Further, a consolidation of the major Federal programs and responsibilities affecting education, I believe, is most desirable and long overdue. A consolidated education effort would afford the Federal Government a greater opportunity to achieve a vital national objective of highest priority--the education of our youth.

Jessie Hopkins Bartlett was the matriarch of the Bartlett family.

ABORTION

In the United States Senate, June 29, 1977

[Senator Bartlett was opposed to abortion.]

A few years ago, this debate on federal funding of discretionary abortions would have been an absurd impossibility. It was generally recognized that abortion is the taking of a human life. This was not a religious issue, not a denominational matter, not a dogmatic statement. It was simple fact. Before this medical procedure, there are two lives. Afterwards, there is only one.

But that has changed. It has become convenient to pretend that abortion is nothing but an operation on a single human being. Were that assertion true, abortion would be no business of the Congress. But, in fact, when we debate this issue on the floor of the Senate, we are discussing nothing less than the federally subsidized extermination of hundreds of thousands of lives.

Albert Schweitzer long ago warned, "If a man loses reverence for any part of life, he will lose his reverence for all life." We have seen that happen with ghastly results in one country after another. Now I fear it is occurring in our own country.

Public officials have dared to argue that it is cheaper for the federal government to abort a baby than to pay its mother additional welfare. How long will it take them to figure out how much cheaper it would be for Medicaid to hasten the death of the aged and infirm rather than support them in nursing homes?

Last year, when this same issue was before us, it was solemnly argued that it would be unconstitutional to deny to poor women the "right" to abort discovered by the Supreme Court in 1973. I doubt we will hear that argument today, for the Court has recently made clear that neither the states nor the federal government have any obligation to pay for elective abortions. It has taken the court eight months to reach that decision. And all the while, because of the personal preference of a singly judge, federal funds have continued to pay for the elimination of certain unwanted Americans.

Dewey treasured the moments he spent on the ranch.

The House of Representatives has already taken appropriate action to continue the prohibition of federal funding of discretionary abortions. The Senate should concur. It would be a tragic mistake to force tens of millions of taxpayers to pay for an act which is, to them, nothing short of murder. The Supreme Court has assured us we need not do it. And I hope our conscience will tell us we should not do it.

I strongly support the amendment offered by the Senator from North Carolina which would maintain in Fiscal 1978 the same prohibition against federal funding of discretionary abortions which the Congress legislated last year.

Mr. and Mrs. Alfred Dewey Follett
request the honour of your
presence at the marriage of their daughter
Jessie Hopkins
to
Mr. David Albert Bartlett
on Tuesday, the twenty-sixth of December
at eight o'clock in the evening
at Saint Luke's Church
Marietta, Ohio

1916 wedding announcement of David Albert Bartlett and Jessie Hopkins.

TRIBUTE TO HUBERT HUMPHREY

In the United States Senate, January 24, 1978)

[Hubert Humphrey of Minnesota was a longtime member of the United States Senate before he was vice president under Lyndon Johnson. He ran twice unsuccessfully for president]

Mr. President, while Hubert Humphrey was never President of the United States, he was a leader of our country in other ways. He was a model to everyone on Capitol Hill as well as to people across the Nation.

Senator Humphrey was usually the keystone of the liberals, and I was usually in opposition to his ideological approach. Yet I always admired the man for his courage to speak and act on his convictions. When there is a critical issue at stake, there will be at least two opinions, each of which needs to be evaluated and clarified. It is healthy and productive to debate these issues on the Senate floor, and Senator Humphrey was one of the best at presenting and defending the ideals in which he believed.

Hubert Humphrey gained the love of virtually every American in his final days. His zest for life, his appealing qualities as a human being became examples for all of us to emulate. His optimism in spite of disappointment, his determination to succeed in the shadow of overwhelming circumstances, and his witty sense of humor when most of us would have given up, have left an impression on all of us.

Senator Humphrey's accomplishments include his battle for civil rights, initiation of the Peace Corps, and the establishment of the food-for-peace program. So many of the issues he fervently fought for will continue to be vital issues for years to come. Hubert Humphrey's causes and style will long be remembered in Congress, and his position as a revered, humanitarian statesman will be etched in our history and in our hearts.

Dewey was joined by his family on the campaign trail.

URBAN POLICY

In the United States Senate, April 20, 1978

[Bartlett disagreed with those who thought lots of federal money was the only salvation for America's decaying urban areas.]

Mr. President, as the June 30 expiration date for the New York City Seasonal Loan Act approaches, debate on basic American urban policy will intensify. I welcome this increased dialogue and the chance it affords Americans to consider the fundamentals of the relationship that should exist between the Federal Government and State and local governments.

The pronouncements of many of the nation's mayors, as well as the recently announced "new partnership" urban policy of President [Jimmy] Carter, have accustomed us to demands for billions of dollars of Federal taxpayers' money to "save the cities." We hear from all sides that the nations' large cities are struggling for their very existence, that their survival is at stake. It would serve the public interest much better if the hysterics and exaggerated language were dropped and it was admitted that what we are facing is a choice, not a crisis. The American people are reflecting new realities by voting down increased school levies, as in Ohio, and by moving away, as in New York City.

Most of the problems that the cities face are problems that Federal money or programs can do little to resolve. Strained budgets, rising crime rates, economic stagnation, nightmare unemployment, and poverty are not problems that are so easily solved by the Federal Government as the mayors and the President seem to think. In 1954, total Federal aid to States and local governments was about $3 billion. In 1976, the total had increased to over $59 billion--from $3 billion to $59 billion in only 22 years. These years span the time in which the so-called crisis of the cities reached major dimensions--Federal involvement has not noticeably slowed this process, and, in fact, in some cases it has demonstrably increased the deterioration of some cities.

Many of our nation's mayors apparently live in a dream world in which they think that Federal money is all they need to solve their problems. They must wake up to the fact that most of their problems are being brought about by shifting socioeconomic relationships, and that cities are in a period of transition. Many of them must face the fact that Americans are voting with their feet, and thereby undercutting the economic base of their cities.

New York City is a prime, or perhaps the prime, example of this deteriorating economic base. During the 1960s, private sector employment in the city grew only 2 percent, compared to almost 27 percent in the entire country. During that decade, U.S. employment in manufacturing grew about 7 percent, but it declined in New York City by 19 percent, representing a loss of 180,000 jobs.

Since 1970 the city has experienced a drastic decline in employment, with a loss of 468,000 jobs, just over an 11 percent decrease in employment. Since 1969 manufacturing employment has fallen at an annual average rate of 48,000 jobs. Total population between 1970 and 1975 decreased in New York City by 5.2 percent. As a General Accounting Office study sagely points out--The prospects for halting this trend are not bright.

The question arises whether the Federal Government should even by trying to reverse this trend. After all, the situation has arisen because of the free choice of

American citizens reacting to changing economic and political realities. I am firmly convinced that no good will be accomplished trying to prohibit these fundamental changes from taking place by damming up the cities with Federal dollars and trying to halt the flowing times. By trying to do so we only treat symptoms, not causes, and we make the final reckoning worse.

Conservatives, such as myself, are often accused of being naysayers because we criticize those who want to spend taxpayers' money on programs ostensibly designed to help the cities and their residents. The fact is, we are not the naysayers to change. It is, rather, those people who wish to spend other people's money to maintain the cities as they have been who are the naysayers. As the demographic situation changes, and as the socioeconomic choices made by people change, we are seeing the emergence of new forms of economic organization within political structures that have not changed fast enough to keep pace. As real as many of the problems cities face are, most of them are problems of transition, not of survival. They are problems of choice, not of ultimatums, so that most of the cries to "save the cities" are nothing more than cries of "wolf." The times are changing, and cities as we have traditionally known them may in fact, by dying. That does not mean there need to be any catastrophes or tragedies. It only means we must be flexible.

The complexities and dislocations of change are very real, but my conviction is that the flexibility necessary for an adequate response resides in the lowest level of our national organization, that is, with the local and State governments. Where the cities and States have failed to take the initiative in planning, in reacting to a changing tax base, and in facing the needs of the future, the Federal Government has in the past and can continue in the future to try to assist cities by helping them coordinate their activities and by taking into account the urban effects of Federal actions. However, the Federal Government can be of most help to our cities by undertaking policies to stop inflation and prevent its rekindling, not by yielding to demands to introduce jerrybuilt dams into the stream of changing economic reality.

It has become a tired old song that we conservatives are not responsive to the problems and concerns of ordinary people. The fact is, we are deeply concerned. Our concern springs from a sincere compassion and empathy for the situation of ordinary people. That does not imply that we are blind to reality, as many of our liberal friends appear to be.

Compassion, packaged in the sweet-smelling wrappings of unkeepable promises, unfilled hopes, and other people's money, is not compassion at all, but deception. The compassion of a conservative garbs itself in the robes of constructive compromise, self-reliance, personal dignity, personal responsibility, and a social conscience that recognizes the proper limits of Federal power and jurisdiction. We conservatives are, in fact, the true liberals in the sense of supporting individual liberty and responsibility, while the so-called liberals are ever-ready to impose their particular version of social justice onto the rest of us.

SEVER RELATIONS WITH CUBA

In the United States Senate, June 9, 1978

Mr. President, for several years I have maintained a keen interest in the affairs of Africa the newly founded nations. On several occasions, I have been fortunate enough to journey there and receive a first-hand account of the trials that fledging African nations must weather, while securing a stable economic and political system.

Naturally I have viewed the recent events in Africa with great concern and apprehension. It seems obvious even to the most casual observer, that there is a rising tide in Africa, which if not tempered or arrested, will only foster further chaos and deny the nations of Africa their right of self determination and the opportunity for economic prosperity, that they so desperately need.

Mr. President, the tide of which I am speaking is the escalating Soviet-backed Cuban military presence in Africa, which has repeatedly demonstrated its aggressive intention to disrupt and interfere with the internal affairs of African nations. I would submit to my colleagues that this military presence, of then taking the form of active combat, not only threatens the secure borders of African states but also presents national security challenges to the United States and other nations of the west.

The record of Cuba, as surrogate to Soviet designs, is one of repeated military agitation not only on the African continent but in our own hemisphere as well. In fact, it was in the face of American opposition, that Cuba abandoned its program fostering Communist insurgency to Latin American and turned its attention to greener pastures in Africa, where there was considerably less of an American presence.

It is not my purpose here to build a case against the Cubans. The Cubans have done that for themselves.

Cuba currently maintains thousands of troops in Angola and Ethiopia, where it continues to intervene in the domestic affairs of those nations. The tenuous internal settlement in Rhodesia who seeks to replace a longstanding minority regime, with a government founded on majority rule, faces its only real opposition from terrorist forces trained and supplied by Cuba and the Soviet Union. Additionally, Cuba maintains military personnel and advisors in 12 other African nations, besides the ones I have just mentioned, whose placement can only serve to threaten the security of their neighbors.

The most recent episode where Cuban forces were heavily implicated, bespeaks the nature of Cuba's current role in Africa. In the Shaba Province of Zaire innocent nationals, both black and white, were massacred, private property was looted or destroyed, and Zaire's copper mining operation, which supplies 70 percent of the world's cobalt was shut down indefinitely. To round out the shameful debacle, the President of the United States and the American people, according to our best intelligence reports, were lied to by the leader of the Cuban Government

In my own humble estimation, it is time that the United States resorts to more than rhetoric in dealing with the Cubans. Today I place before the Congress a concurrent resolution urging the President of the United States to take tangible diplomatic, yet peaceful steps, designed to discourage Cuba and the Soviet Union from further military activity in Africa.

Mr. President, I call for the sense of the Senate and the House of Representatives that President Jimmy Carter sever existing diplomatic and economic relations with Cuba and stem any other official acts toward the normalization of relations with Cuba, until such time as Cuba removes combat military forces from Africa.

Since early 1977, there have been significant movements toward re-establishing normalized diplomatic relations with Cuba; the most important to date being the exchange of notes of May 30, 1977. This informal agreement provided interest sections for the United States in the Swiss Embassy in Havana, and for the Cubans in the Czechoslovakian Embassy here in Washington.

The recent movements for normalized political and economic relations have not developed out of a 17-year hiatus without cause. The Cuban economy is in shambles. Cuban officials have actively courted American business in hopes of rebuilding tourism, foreign investment, and trade opportunities.

Eighty-five percent of Cuban foreign exchange earnings are derived from sugar; and given the depressed price of sugar on the international exchange, their economy has fared poorly. Plans for industrial and agricultural diversification have failed. Cuba continues to have the highest per capita foreign indebtedness of any country in Latin America, with over 40 percent of its yearly foreign exchange earnings in hard currency going to pay the interest and principal on its external debt. They would like to see the flow of American dollars into their country continue and increase. They would be hurt if the current flow was stopped and disheartened at the prospect of not having more American dollars.

The President of the United States, in stemming normalized relations with Cuba, would establish the first primary linkage between Cuba's military presence in Africa and their desire for political and economic favor with the West. Mr. Fidel Castro must learn, as any other reasonable participant in the world community, that he cannot have his cake and eat it too. He must be told that Cuban forces cannot go marauding through Africa without sacrificing diplomatic and trade relations he is seeking at home.

Perhaps in the meantime, Mr. Castro might learn that he can best solve his unemployment problems by promoting trade and industry at home instead of shipping soldiers abroad to interfere in the affairs of African nations.

Visiting one evening with the Industrial Editors of Tulsa are Jennifer and Jack High, Bill and Margaret Patterson, and Dewey and Ann Bartlett, 1969.

HASTE MAKES WASTE IN ENERGY POLICY

In opposition to the Energy Act of 1978, in the United States Senate, July 14, 1978

Mr. President, I rise in opposition to the report of the conference on this bill. I opposed the bill in committee and on the floor. While I have worked at every turn—constructively, I hope—to improve the legislation and make its effects more reasonable and less punitive for the area of the country I represent, I do not believe this effort has been fully successful. Although a number of modifications have been made to meet the points I have raised and the legislation has been improved in these respects, it is still far from perfected.

Unfortunately, the work of the conference has also now been marred by the unseemly haste to consider this report and pass a bill simply for show--apparently so that the President [Jimmy Carter] can point in Bonn [West Germany] to the action that will have been taken on his energy program. While it would be nice to be polite, I feel it is essential that someone have the courage to stand up and point out that this effort is a farce.

It is not even a suitable symbol. Were the entire administration energy program put in place, it is unlikely that it would save a single barrel of oil or cubic foot of gas. In fact, it would probably end up decreasing the amount of oil and gas we would otherwise have available, and thereby increase our imports.

Mr. President, this legislation is unnecessary, burdensome, and anticonsumer. In addition, it will increase our consumption of foreign oil. The bill is unnecessary because the laws of economics are driving users away from natural gas as fuel. The bill simply represents an additional blanket of Federal controls designed to address problems created by an earlier, ill-fated layer of Federal controls. Deregulation of new natural gas and decontrol of domestically produced crude oil will alleviate the supply shortfalls this bill is purported to address.

Under this legislation, new industrial boilers and new electric powerplants will not be able to use natural gas or oil unless there is essentially no alternative for environmental or similar reasons. But that is already the case. For economic reasons alone, industry is perfectly capable of making those decisions.

It is business. It is most essential for making a profit for a business to recognize which fuel it should use for the long pull, which is economically in its best interests, which can be used for a long enough time to amortize a very sizable investment, so later on it will not be outlawed because of environmental or other Federal regulatory reasons.

No new powerplants are being built to burn natural gas, but those that exist--and in this area is dependent on them--in Oklahoma, Texas, New Mexico, Louisiana, and a few other States are now being paid for by the consumers of electricity in those States. It is monstrously punitive to compel these States and their consumers to throw these plants away by 1990 and to build new ones, so that relatively small amounts of natural gas could be saved and presumably transported north and east to heat someone's store at a low, controlled price.

This bill is excessively burdensome. A massive regulatory bureaucracy is established to wreak havoc on utilities and industry and cost millions of taxpayer dollars in the process. This bureaucracy will ultimately publish thousands of pages of regulations and case records to monitor what would have happened anyway.

This legislation is anticonsumer oriented. Due to

premature plant retirements and unnecessary cost increases brought about by this bill, utility ratepayers in this country will pay billions of dollars in excess electricity bills. A greatly disproportionate share of the burden will fall on the ratepayers of the Southwest and South. It is estimated that the capital costs of converting existing as-fired generating capacity in Oklahoma to coal capability will be $4 billion and will be passed on to consumers in my State.

This bill will increase our imports of foreign oil. Forced off natural gas, utilities, and industry will not convert existing physical facilities designed to burn natural gas to coal-burning or nuclear capability. Due to economics and institutional barriers, existing generating facilities will be converted wherever possible to oil-burning capability. Since domestic refiners are presently unable to meet domestic fuel oil demand, any increase in demand must be supplied by imports. The resulting adverse impacts on the value of the dollar and on our national security are already well known.

So here we are, with the one source of energy that is available in large amounts, estimated to be a supply for 200 years or so, which we are not utilizing in any way at all to the fullest.

This act is not needed because industry already is converting to oil. No new baseload electrical powerplants utilizing oil or natural gas are being planned. Industry is more concerned with security of supply than with cost of the supplies; to a large extent because oil and gas, especially gas, viewed as likely to be cut off, no new plants are being constructed for their use.

Mr. President, this conference report deserves closer analysis than has been permitted. It is a new document, unlike either original piece of legislation from the House of Representatives or the Senate, and it comprises over

80 legal-size, fine-print pages of highly technical language. It consists of over 40,000 words. It was drafted in secret and kept unavailable to members of the conference and the public until less than 48 hours ago. I might say the conference considered this legislation and approved it in memo or outline form but not in bill form. So this has not been scrutinized very carefully, and it would be my best guess that there are a number of areas in it which would not express adequately or accurately the thinking of some of the conferees who have supported it. I think that there will be in this legislation a number of provisions that will be political nightmares to those who administer the legislation.

Mr. President, I urge my colleagues to oppose this legislation. I do not think that it is in the best interests of the Nation. It certainly is not fair to the State of Oklahoma, which I represent, and which will be paying a very large and disproportionate share of the forced conversion costs.

AMERICA'S ENERGY PROBLEM

In the United States Senate, September 20, 1978

The "energy problem" has been a focus of national concern since the 1973 Arab Oil Embargo. Unfortunately, it has been treated as a mysterious problem, somehow divorced from all other human experience. This is not so. Rather, we have had a short-term shock, in the midst of a long-term mishandling of the energy situation, primarily by the Federal Government. The Congress and various administrations, who share the blame, in turn, protect themselves by blaming the oil and gas industry.

Similarly, some have approached the situation in more cosmic terms, saying, "We have passed out of the era of cheap and abundant energy." I do not believe the facts support this idea. When you discount for inflation, most forms of energy are cheaper at the retail level today than they were 20 years ago. Many are cheaper than 10 years ago. And although the 1973-74 price increases did administer a severe shock to our system, oil, gasoline and electricity prices have been stable in real terms since then, as the market system, although constrained, has been able to work.

In 1942, my mother and I bought a new Ford with a sticker price of $690.00. Gasoline was 19 cents/gallon. Today a Ford LTD costs $5,390.00 and gasoline averages 61.7 cents/gallon. Ford has gone up over 7 1/2 times, gasoline less than 3 1/2 times. Both, of course, are greatly improved in quality.

Relatively speaking, the price of energy has fallen almost continuously over the past 200 years. And so, while I have no doubts that gas and oil will eventually "run out", it will only be in the sense that newer energy sources have been developed that will be more economical and efficient to use than the remaining oil and gas deposits.

So, what is to blame for our recent energy difficulties? To understand the situation, you must recall that oil and gas production is a long-term proposition. The oil we use today is largely the result of discoveries made 10-15 years ago.

In 1956, over 58,000 wells were drilled in the United States looking for oil and gas. Drilling then entered a long period of decline, finally hitting rock bottom in 1971 and 1973 when less than 28,000 wells were drilled. Thus, even though production of oil and gas rose throughout the 1960's, we were sowing the seeds of our present problems. And even though drilling and finding have risen dramatically in response to increased prices since 1973, 1978 will probably see only a little over 50,000 wells drilled. Perhaps, by 1979, we will have reached the level of drilling effort we had in 1956. But the domestic demand for gas and oil today is more than twice that of 1956 and both are harder to find, deeper, and more expensive to find.

Just reflect on that. What would be your opinion of the health of the auto industry if it produced today only the same number of cars as in 1955? Or agriculture if we produced no more food than we did 20 years ago. So in this perspective, the major reason for a problem with oil and gas production and exploration is that we just have not been trying as hard as we could.

And why not? The answer is primarily government controls and action. In 1954, the Supreme Court placed price controls on interstate gas production, bringing considerable confusion and uncertainty to exploration for gas. In the case of natural gas, we have had practically a laboratory experiment. Because the Supreme Court's decision rested on a law governing interstate commerce, the extension of regulation did not reach gas produced and consumed within the same state. There thus arose an intrastate gas market, free of controls, side by side with the controlled market.

Under free market conditions, the intrastate market prospered. Each year, the amount of gas found through new exploration just about equaled the amount being used. Total production in the intrastate market has continued to increase, even during the last few years when total gas production declined. And there were no shortages in the intrastate market.

The experience in the controlled market was quite different. Since 1970, total production in that market has declined. In fact, by 1976, gas reserves in the interstate market were only about half of what they were a decade earlier. In addition, the interstate market has been subject to grave shortages. At the artificially low prices of recent years, consumers have wanted to use lots of natural gas, frequently for wasteful purposes, while producers have had little incentive to produce. In the free intrastate market, it has been quite the opposite. Realistic prices for gas have lead to conservation, while production has been enhanced.

The one most frequently heard argument against free enterprise is that "It's too expensive." In the short-term, it is true, it is possible to keep prices down by using up reserves while depressing new exploration. But in the long-run, the society is going to have to pay the costs associated with finding new energy, if they want to use that energy. The fact that we have "shortages" now means that people are willing pay high OPEC [Organization of Petroleum Exporting Countries] prices for imported oil to obtain what they need.

The problem is a shortage of energy--not high prices to the poor and those on low fixed incomes. We are currently importing forty percent of our current oil consumption--about 7 million bbls. Even in terms of the effect of energy prices on the poor, artificially low prices are not a solution. To the extent the poor and those on low fixed incomes should be subsidized, it should be a subsidy related to their needs, not to the level of their energy use and at the expense of adequate domestic energy supplies and sensible conservation.

A second argument made is that oil and gas companies are monopolies which will reap "excess profits" if a free market price is allowed. Measured as a percentage of return on capital, however, the petroleum industry has been almost exactly in line with the average for all American business, when measured over any reasonable period of time. If Congress, sitting in the cat bird seat, would decide that new profits were not spent on exploration and development, it could increase taxes on energy companies at anytime.

And few industries are actually as competitive as oil and gas production. In virtually every phase of the industries, the top 8 companies have barely 50% of the business in any particular activity. Compare this with autos, steel, soup, computers or what-have-you, and you find far less concentration in oil and gas.

Finally, there is the argument that higher prices simply will not bring results. Here I would again point to the intrastate market where higher prices, fair prices, have brought results.

Now, I'd like to talk a little bit about oil, because the situations in oil and gas are different in some important respects. In the early 1970s, the gas market was about 40% free, while the oil market was entirely free, expect for the effects of the oil import program. However, with the imposition of price controls by President [Richard] Nixon in 1971, followed by the Emergency Petroleum

Allocation Act in 1973 and the Energy Production and Conservation Act in 1975, oil came under overwhelming and universal control. There is no free intrastate market in oil to allow a contrast. And as you might expect, oil production under controls has suffered. One of the few bright spots has been the so-called "stripper" oil program. This allows the sale of oil at uncontrolled prices if it comes from wells producing less than 10 barrels per day. Once a well is so classified, if the operator can use new techniques to raise production, he does not lose the benefits of free market pricing. A little over one-eighth of American production now comes from stripper wells, and that was held steady, while other categories have declined.

Many of us in the Senate have been supporting what we call a "deep stripper" amendment, which would allow stripper treatment for wells producing larger amounts of oil, if they are at greater depths. If this amendment is adopted, about another one-eighth of production can be freed from controls. This would enable production at near its economic limit, to produce mush longer and in some cases, to be increased by enhanced recovery methods.

There are many, many techniques that can be used to expand production, but they cannot be used under current regulated prices. Wells that appear played out can be made to flow again by waterflooding and other secondary and tertiary recovery techniques. But these operations cannot take place at the price of $5.25 per barrel that is now allowed for old oil. So we see the strange sight of American production being shut in or plugged because we can't pay more than $5.25 for it, while we are cheerfully paying $14 and more for imports. It just doesn't make sense.

With many of the things I have said thus far, I am

sure my good friend Jim Abourezk will disagree. I'd like to finish up my talk on a topic on which we do agree, and that is the Natural Gas Bill now pending before the Senate. It seems strange to some that we should be on the same side of this issue, but I think that is explained by what we have in common. I think we can agree, as Senator Long has said, that this bill is like a two-headed horse, trying to ride off in two different directions. It tries to espouse the philosophy of deregulation while imposing a regime of incredibly complex regulation. Senator Abourezk would like complete regulation and I want complete deregulation. The bill does neither.

A brief summary of the bill is totally impossible, so I will merely give a few of the high points. The bill immediately places control on all gas, so that the over 40% of the gas market that is now free--the intrastate market--will disappear for at least 7 years, possible 8 1/2 years. When "deregulation" does occur in 1985, less than 40% of the domestic gas then producing will be deregulated, less than is unregulated now.

Some Senators who supported the Pearson-Bentsen bill--a deregulation bill--said they were willing to have at least 7 years of total price controls if eventually we have deregulation. But we won't have deregulation with this conference report.

During the period between now and 1985, gas will be subject to a bewildering variety of price categories. Even gas that is "new" in the sense that it is produced by putting down your drill bit next week will be subject to at least 5 difference prices, and the producer may not know which one he will get until he finds the gas, and until long regulatory proceedings are held at both the state and federal level.

Under the present system, the intrastate market is free, while even in the interstate market, whatever gas you find comes under the single price set by the Federal Energy Regulatory Commission based on the cost of finding gas during that particular period.

Although the bill is now touted by the administration as a "deregulation bill", even in 1985, after deregulation is supposed to occur, less than 40% of gas will be deregulated, or even less than what we have now. This is because only certain categories of narrowly defined gas are deregulated. Equally important, deregulation is only guaranteed for 6 months. After that, the President may reimpose controls simply by signing an order, and he may be overridden only by an affirmative vote of both Houses of Congress.

We see this as a bill that will not provide additional gas supply. It places controls on the uncontrolled market, and exchanges a system of regulation on the interstate market which is at least well understood for one that is equally stringent but totally unknown and unworkable. Nor will this bill advance the dollar or our international prestige. If the bill is a bad bill, it is very hard to believe that foreigners will not see through it in very short order.

Milton Friedman, the Nobel-prize-winning economist, said recently in a letter to our committee: "In any event, the dollar has not been weak because of the energy problem, and no amount of tinkering with energy legislation will have any significant or lasting effect on the dollar. The dollar is weak because of bad economic policy, policy which is destroying the unrivaled capacity for growth of American free enterprise...policy which is producing inflation through excessive government spending and excessive creation of money." And I would note that Canada, which is a net exporter of energy, has seen its dollar fall even against the American dollar in the last year.

Ann Bartlett surrounded by her children and grandchildren, 1990. Top row: Susan Bartlett, and Tom Atkinson, Middle row: Kate Atkinson, Ann Bartlett Burke, and Joanie Atkinson, Bottom row: Annie Atkinson; Dewey Bartlett III, and Dewey Bartlett, Jr.

This amendment provides as a general rule that no funds shall be obligated or expended to administer or enforce any standard, rule, regulation, or order under the Occupational Safety and Health Act of 1970 which would be applicable to small businessmen who employ 10 or fewer employees, and whose industry group has an occupational injury incidence rate of seven or less per hundred full-time employees based upon the annual Bureau of Labor Statistics survey of 3- and 4-digit Standard Industrial Classification Code industries

However, this amendment specifically allows OSHA to conduct investigations to determine the causes of a serious injury or death at such a workplace; it allows OSHA to conduct health inspections as currently done; it allows OSHA to conduct inspections as a result of non-frivolous employee complaints; and it allows employers to participate in whatever OSHA educational or consulting services they wish. It also provides that the injury/incidence rate be based on a survey of 3- and 4-digit SIC Code industries, thereby becoming much more sensitive to the problem of hazardous firms being categorized in a safe industry group. Using random sampling techniques this could be accomplished with no perceptible additional burden in paperwork.

It has been estimated that OSHA is costing American business about $3 billion a year. What are employees getting for this huge outlay? The evidence suggests very little. In the 6 years of OSHA existence through 1977, agency officers had found 1,357,360 violations. Of these 2.8 percent were serious--defined as willful, repeated and imminent danger--and 97.2 percent were nonserious. Does anyone need Federal agency giving fines for torn screen doors, cracked toilet seats, fire extinguishers inches out of place or for improper agricultural drainage when the standing water was the

So, this bill is bad on its merits, will have no favorable effect on our economic condition, and should be rejected. Sen. Jim Abourezk and I both want to kill parts of the conference report—and we plan to accomplish this with a motion to recommit. We will add instructions to the recommital motion which would authorize the President to: (1) declare an emergency and then to price and allocate natural gas; and, (2) with approval by the Federal Energy Regulatory Commission [FERC], authorize an intrastate pipeline to sell to an interstate pipeline or utility without coming under federal jurisdiction. Our alternative proposal would assure that all uncommitted or unused gas can reach an interstate consumer in need. This legislation, coupled with the setting of reasonable prices for 1977-78 and 1979-80 by FERC could increase substantially the domestic natural gas supplies available to the interstate market. The potential involved here can be seen in earlier pricing decisions by the Federal Power Commission. Price increases to 52 cents in late 1974, and up to $1.42 in 1976, resulted in an increase in dedications to 3 trillion cubic feet in 1976 and to 8.6 trillion cubic feet in 1977. The passage of our alternative to the Natural Gas Conference Report, accompanied by pricing incentives by FERC, would constitute a very good interim solution.

For the long run, the Congress as a whole should do what the Senate has twice done--pass a simple and fundamental new gas deregulation bill. The Pearson-Bentsen substitute, passed by the Senate a year ago, provided for immediate new gas deregulation with an interim price ceiling for two years onshore and five years offshore. Just as important, it left the free and vital intrastate natural gas market intact. The only workable way to alleviate our long-term gas supply problems is to eliminate regulation, not expand it: to build upon the freedom of the intrastate market and provide for simple, general deregulation of new natural gas in a reasonable period of time.

Dewey and his mother Jessie Follett, at one-year.

LIMIT OSHA

In the United States Senate, September 2

Mr. President, I am offering an amendmen end the use of Federal money by OSHA (Oc Safety and Health Administration) to harass safe small businesses. This amendment is a compromise of an amendment I offered on Au Small Business Committee bill which was pas Senate by a vote of 51 to 42. I point out, Mr. that this amendment includes the amendme duced before plus the so-called Conti-Bartl ment that was introduced in the conference and to my knowledge answers all the que have been raised about it.

The original amendment would have ex small businesses that employ 10 or fewer emp that have an injury/illness incidence rate of se per hundred from OSHA regulation. I wo point out that OSHA considers a nine injury/ dence rate as the breaking point between haz non-hazardous businesses and companies.

Even though the Senate did pass that ver amendment the Small Business Committee rejected it. In order to meet the objections raised against the original version of the am House Members, I have revised the amendr form I offer it in today.

The intent of this amendment is very sim the spending of Federal money to nit-pick small businesses that are already extreme other words, to bring a little common sens effectiveness into the implementation of our safety laws.

result of employees just having washed their cars?

I would also say that this amendment will tend to reduce inflation, because it will reduce the cost of doing business of many small businesses, and at the same time it will provide an incentive for them to conduct their operations in a safer, less hazardous way, and it will give them incentive to be more productive, to increase their productivity. This will certainly help the problem of inflation.

It cannot even be shown that OSHA has accomplished anything other than inflation. National Safety Council statistics show that job related deaths have been on a steady decline since 1937--without OSHA. The council's figures also show that the worst year since 1940 for job related injuries was in 1973--2 years after OSHA had been created. One of the recommendations that a House Committee on Small Business report on OSHA made was to "assign high priority to the shift in resources away from low risk businesses toward higher risk businesses," just what I am attempting to accomplish with this amendment.

This will enable OSHA to utilize its manpower to a more efficient extent, by concentrating on those businesses of 10 and under employees which are the hazardous ones--and there are some--and to improve their situation, rather than spending time with businesses that have no incidence at all, or a very low incidence, of injuries per thousand.

I might add that this amendment enjoys very broad support from the American small business community, those who are employed by the small businesses, and all those who bear the burden of unnecessary regulations when regulation is translated into higher consumer prices, increased inflation, and increased unemployment.

Ann spent many hours tending to her garden, 1960.

REMARKS BY U.S. DISTRICT JUDGE RALPH THOMPSON AT DEWEY BARTLETT'S ENSHRINEMENT INTO THE OKLAHOMA AIR SPACE HALL OF FAME

Oklahoma City, November 11, 1986

Six months after the Japanese attack on Pearl Harbor, Dewey F. Bartlett, president of the senior class, addressed his classmates at the Princeton graduation ceremony. It was a patriotic speech, Virtually every able bodied graduate was bound for military service. Dewey Bartlett entered the Naval Aviation Cadet Program, earned his wings and was commissioned a second lieutenant in the Marine Corps. He completed advanced training in the SBD, the Douglass Dauntless dive bomber, at El Toro Marine Air Station, California. He sailed to Hawaii on the aircraft carrier *Kitty Hawk* and deployed to the Johnston Islands. There he moved to Espiritu Santo and flew strikes against Japanese targets at Bougainville and New Britain. Next, he and his squadron flew dive bombing missions in close support of ground troops in the invasion of Luzon at Lingayen Gulf, Philippine Islands. Military historians, citing his squadron's performance, have called these missions a milestone in Marine aviation because of the success of the extremely close air support of infantry. It facilitated the drive down Luzon to re-capture Manila. Often, the Marine dive bombers were the ground forces' only cover. He was awarded the Air Medal, his squadron a Navy Unit Citation, but the greatest praise and recognition came from the ground troops themselves. The commanding general of the First Calvary Division was lavish in his praise of the Marine dive bomber pilots supporting their advances.

Following the war, Dewey Bartlett entered the oil business in Tulsa in which he enjoyed much success. He was public spirited and unselfish, being elected to the Oklahoma State Senate and later Governor of Oklahoma. In 1972, he was elected United States Senator from Oklahoma. His administration and distinguished service are remembered for his intelligence, hard work, business-like approach, stubbornness when high standards were involved, and complete integrity. Until his death he continued his love of flying. His Bonanza was well known among air fields large and small throughout the state. He talked flying, literally, with fuel hands at grass strips and with Presidents of the United States.

His hand on the stick, as on the ship of state, was always strong, always sure, always steady. He was sound and smart and courageous--good qualities for pilots - good qualities for people. He was a statesman and an aviator in the highest traditions of both.

He would have been immensely honored to be in your company tonight, and to be honored in this most extraordinary way. In his absence, Dewey Bartlett, Jr., will accept the award.

INDEX

H

J

K

L